RACE AND POVERTY

THE ECONOMICS OF DISCRIMINATION

Edited by John F. Kain

 PRENTICE-HALL, Inc., Englewood Cliffs, N.J.

JOHN F. KAIN, the editor of this volume in the Modern Economic Issues series, is Professor of Economics at Harvard University. He is co-author of *Urban Transportation Problem* and has written numerous professional articles on urban problems.

To Mary Fan, Mary Jo, and Joanna

Current printing (last number):
10 9 8 7 6 5 4 3 2 1

PRENTICE-HALL INTERNATIONAL, INC. (*London*)
PRENTICE-HALL OF AUSTRALIA, PTY. LTD. (*Sydney*)
PRENTICE-HALL OF CANADA, LTD. (*Toronto*)
PRENTICE-HALL OF INDIA PRIVATE LIMITED (*New Delhi*)
PRENTICE-HALL OF JAPAN, INC. (*Tokyo*)

PREFACE

It is now commonplace to identify race and poverty as the two major problems confronting American society today. This book is vitally concerned with both, and particularly with the way in which racial discrimination affects Negro poverty.

The editor's introduction provides a brief survey of the current economic condition of the Negro American and an examination of the major historical and contemporary factors responsible for the present gap between the economic position of Negro and white Americans. The readings that follow are concerned principally with contemporary factors and are divided into five parts: the economic condition of the Negro; labor market discrimination; housing market discrimination; attitudes: white and black; and policy alternatives: black capitalism, ghetto development, integration.

In the course of writing my introduction and selecting the papers to be included, I received helpful suggestions from H. James Brown, Joseph J. Persky, Eric A. Hanushek, and Otto Eckstein. I would like to thank them for their comments, all of which improved the book. Finally, I would like to thank Mrs. Molly R. Mayo and Mrs. Anna Bell for their sizable contributions in preparing both the introductory essay and the complete manuscript.

J.F.K.

CONTENTS

v

INTRODUCTION

RACE AND POVERTY: THE ECONOMICS OF DISCRIMINATION

John F. Kain

The gap between Negro and white economic conditions has been of long duration, its roots firmly buried in the institution of slavery. Lincoln could free the Negro people from slavery with the stroke of a pen, but he could not so easily free them from its ruinous legacies. Even if they had been given every opportunity, the former slaves were not prepared by training or experience to function effectively as freedmen. The victorious North did too little to insure the new citizens' rights and economic self-sufficiency, and the defeated and embittered South did too much to emasculate both. In the decades following the Civil War, an already disadvantaged people had to endure continuing and intense discrimination in education, employment, housing, and voting. Against these odds, the progress of the American Negro in the century since emancipation must be considered a significant achievement.

The nation's entry into World War I marked the beginning of a new and more hopeful era for the Negro American in the "promised land."[1] The expanding industries of Northern cities held out the promise of better jobs and a freer life. Millions were to make the journey in the half-century that followed. Although reality often fell considerably short of the promise, the economic position of the Negro slowly improved in the less restrictive climate of Northern cities. Perhaps more importantly, as the black populations of Northern cities continued to increase, the Negro acquired a growing voice in national affairs. This broadened political base made possible the return of the Federal presence to the South in support of Negro rights.

This essay examines the historical and contemporary factors that are responsible for the income gap between Negro and white Americans. It begins with a brief survey of the current economic position of Negroes and whites and the evidence of Negro economic progress, both absolute and relative to that of whites, reviews the historical factors that explain part of these income differences, and examines recent quantitative estimates of the cost of discrimination. This leads naturally to a consideration of the contemporary factors that have perpetuated Negro and white differences, specifically inadequate investment in Negro education, discrimination in employment, and discrimination in housing. The essay ends with a review of the alternative strategies that have been proposed to improve the economic position of the Negro and overcome discrimination.

THE ECONOMIC CONDITION OF THE NEGRO AMERICAN

In every sphere of American life the economic condition of the Negro minority is inferior to that of the white majority. In 1967 an estimated 35 per cent of all nonwhite persons belonged to spending units (families and unrelated individuals) with incomes below the poverty level.[2] This was an incidence of poverty three and one half times greater than that found among whites. Admittedly this represents a considerable reduction in Negro poverty as compared to a decade ago. In 1959 (the first year in which this particular Poverty Index was computed), over half (55 per cent) of all nonwhite persons belonged to spending units with incomes below the poverty level. Similarly, in the past decade the median family income of nonwhites increased by 83 per cent; from $2,764 in 1957 to $5,177 in 1967. Even allowing for inflation, real nonwhite family income increased by 58 per cent.[3] The Negro American has thus benefited from the growing productivity of the national economy.

How can these rapid declines in the incidence of Negro poverty and equally rapid increases in Negro incomes be reconciled with the widespread references to a "crisis" and the very real dissatisfaction exhibited by many Negroes? The explanation must be found in the fact that while the absolute condition of the Negro has improved markedly in the last decade, his relative position has improved barely perceptibly. The growth in productivity that has produced rapid increases in Negro incomes and living standards has propelled white Americans to new heights as well. Be it ten years ago or fifty years ago, the economic condition of the Negro American has lagged far behind that of the white American. The gap has closed very little.

During the same eight-year period (1959–1967) in which the incidence of poverty among nonwhites declined from 55 per cent to 35 per cent, the incidence of poverty among whites declined from 18 to 10 per cent. Similarly, while the median family income of nonwhites more than doubled in less than a decade, it changed very little in comparison to the income of white families. Nonwhite median family income as a ratio of that of whites has fluctuated in the range of 51–62 per cent for nearly two decades, becoming more favorable to nonwhites during periods of full employment and deteriorating during recessions.* "Social and Economic Conditions of Negroes in the United States," a report by the Bureau of Labor Statistics and the Bureau of Census, summarizes these and other statistics (pp. 33–37).

That poverty and economic well-being must be thought of in relative terms is illustrated by comparisons of the incomes of the Negro American with those of populations in other parts of the world. Thus, while the 1960 per capita income of the average American Negro is substantially less than that of the average white, it is roughly 13 per cent greater than that of the average Englishman, nearly five times that of the average Spaniard, and more than fifteen times that of the average Nigerian.[4] Indeed even the destitute black sharecroppers of the Mississippi Delta have per capita incomes that exceed the per capita incomes of all but a few countries outside Western Europe.

While the evidence of a significant secular improvement in the relative income position of black Americans in the past decade and a half is meager, there is more substantial evidence of improvement if the beginning of World War II is taken as the initial position. Even though the data are not entirely comparable to those discussed above, it is estimated that the median family income of nonwhite families and individuals was 37 per cent of the white median in 1939.[5] This and other evidence indicates that during the period 1939–1950 Negroes rapidly improved their relative income position nationally. Most of this advance was achieved during World War II when large numbers of Negroes shifted from jobs in Southern agriculture to jobs in Northern industry.

In some respects the progress is not as favorable as it seems. A constant ratio of nonwhite to white family income for the nation as a whole, such as characterized the past decade and a half, implies a worsening relative position for Negroes in each region of the country. As Alan Batchelder points out, only continued high levels of net migration from the poorest and most discriminating parts of the South to Northern metropolitan areas made it possible for Negro males to maintain a relative constancy of income with respect to white males in the decade 1950–1960 (pp. 45–51 of this volume). Between 1949 and 1959, all four census regions showed a decline in the median income of Negro men as a ratio of the median income of white men even though this ratio remained approximately constant for the nation as a

---

* Data on Negro, as contrasted with all nonwhite, incomes have been published for only four years. These statistics indicate that Negro incomes are significantly lower than those of all nonwhites, a finding that is confirmed by other measures. In 1967, when the median family income of all nonwhites was 62 per cent that of whites, the income of Negro families was only 59 per cent.

whole. Interestingly enough, Batchelder discovered that in every region the median incomes of Negro females improved relative to those of white females.

Any attempt to provide a balanced evaluation of the economic status of the Negro would be incomplete if it failed to make some reference to the increasing numbers of Negro families that are managing to achieve middle-class status. Between 1947 and 1960, the percentage of Negro families earning more than $7,000 per year increased from 7 to 17 per cent.[6] In the next six years, 1960 to 1966, the fraction increased to 28 per cent as compared to over 50 per cent of white families. In 1966, 12 per cent of Negro families earned more than $10,000 per year compared to 30 per cent of whites. In some respects discrimination cuts most cruelly against this group of Negro Americans.

The level of Negro incomes relative to whites is strongly dependent on economic conditions. It is commonplace to state that Negroes are the last hired and first fired. Whether or not this is literally true as a description of the actual operations of the labor market, there

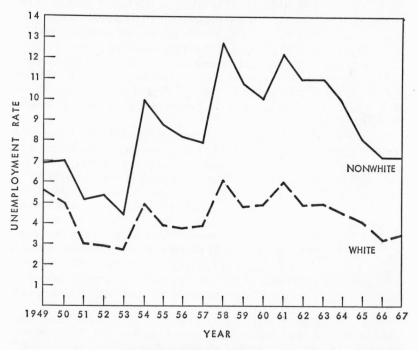

Source: Bureau of Labor Statistics and Bureau of the Census, "Social and Economic Conditions of Negroes in the United States" (October, 1967), p. 30.

Figure 1. *Nonwhite and White Unemployment Rates, 1949–1967.*

is considerable evidence that Negro unemployment rates are strongly influenced by the level of aggregate demand. As illustrated in Figure 1, the rate of Negro unemployment consistently has held at about twice the white level since the end of World War II.[7] The ratio 2:1 seems to hold for virtually all subgroups. For example, during the first nine months of 1967 the unemployment rates for nonwhite married men averaged 3.4 per cent, less than half the rate for all nonwhites. Yet this was still more than twice the rate, 1.6 per cent, for white married men. Indeed a gap of roughly this magnitude is characteristic of virtually every indicator of Negro and white welfare. The task is to explain these persistent differences.

HISTORICAL FACTORS

For analytical purposes, the history of the Negro American may be divided into three periods: pre-Civil War, 1865 to 1940, and 1940 to the present.[8] In the first period Negroes were the essential labor force of the slave system. In the second they largely remained in the rural South as the agricultural labor force of a "free" cotton economy. Since 1940, the demise of cotton and the development of new urban industrial opportunities have fostered a movement to metropolitan areas. This shift, still by no means finished, has brought Negroes to Northern cities in large numbers.

Before the start of World War II nearly eight out of every ten Negroes lived in the states of the Confederacy, a generally poor and economically retarded region, which still had not fully recovered from the devastation and disorganization of the Civil War and its aftermath. In 1940 the South's per capita income was only about 60 per cent of the nation's, and the Negro population was concentrated in the poorest states of the South, such as Mississippi, whose per capita income in the same year was only 37 per cent of the nation's.[9] Despite a rapid regional redistribution of the Negro population since the start of World War II, the concentration of the Negro in low income states remains an important part of the "explanation" of Negro poverty today. More than half of all Negroes still live in the South, and that region continues to lag far behind the rest of the nation in productivity and incomes.

It was also true that Negroes were concentrated in agriculture, a declining, low-wage industry. In 1940 fully a third of all Negro workers were employed in farming compared to about one-sixth of white workers.[10] Few Negro farmers owned the land they worked, and what little land they did own was poor and badly equipped. Typically, Negroes were sharecroppers (tenants) or wage laborers. Although the proportion of the Negro labor force in farming has declined markedly in recent decades, the overrepresentation of the Negro in this sector continues.

The limited number of Negro nonagricultural workers were concentrated in either low-paid service occupations or had menial tasks in industry. Few were skilled workers, and the handicrafts and industries in the South where they had a foothold were declining. The majority of manufacturing industries in the South would not employ Negroes, and Negroes were not numerous in professional, business, or clerical positions in either the South or the North. The few exceptions were those serving exclusively the Negro public. (See the article by Andrew F. Brimmer, pp. 89–99 of this volume.) These patterns of geographic location and occupational specialization remain directly traceable to the regional concentration of the slave population.

Slavery

The economics of slavery is directly responsible for the overrepresentation of Negroes in the South at the end of the Civil War and their even more extreme concentration in Southern agriculture. There had been little use for slaves in the North, and the Northern state governments had not permitted slavery to become an accepted institution. The South, on the other hand, came to regard slavery as an essential part of its economy and imported Africans until the slave trade was made illegal. After 1808, Southerners continued to increase the number of slaves through breeding and smuggling.

There has been a great deal of controversy about the profitability of slavery in the antebellum South and about whether slavery was an efficient and viable form of economic organization. Many writers, especially southern historians, have argued that slavery was not a viable economic system at the time of the Civil War and probably would have destroyed itself within less than a generation. Thus, the war was unnecessary insofar as the slavery issue was concerned. However, Alfred Conrad and John Meyer conclude that the return on investment in slaves was competitive with returns being earned on other capital assets at the same time.[11] They try to show that the product of the labor of the slaves had a value large enough to cover the cost of rearing and maintaining slaves, plus a surplus. The most novel aspect of their analysis is their depiction of the antebellum South as a two-region, two-commodity economy. The newer areas best suited to the production of cotton (and other important staples) specialized in agricultural production, while the older areas, with poorer soil, specialized in the production of slaves, exporting them to the staple-crop areas. This form of specialization and interregional trade made "slavery" profitable to the whole South. The continuing demand for labor in the Cotton Belt insured returns to the slave-breeding operations in the seaboard and border states. The returns from slave breeding (an intermediate good in the slave system) were necessary to make the plantation operations on the poorer lands profitable.

At the outbreak of the War between the States, only a scattering of Negroes lived in the North and practically none lived in the West. A Northern victory and the Emancipation Proclamation removed the legal restrictions on Negro mobility, and in the half century following the Civil War, the proportion of Negroes in the North and West nearly doubled. Even though the proportion nearly doubled again between 1910 and 1940, eight out of every ten Negroes still lived in the South at the start of World War II.

Emancipation and Reconstruction

The first effect of freedom was probably a decline in the standard of living of the Negro. While some efforts were made to help the newly enfranchised American toward self-sufficiency, they were hopelessly inadequate for the enormously difficult task of preparing the former slaves for a new role in the economic system. An estimated 80 per cent of Negroes were totally illiterate and most were landless and destitute. The rumor, widely circulated among freedmen, that the Federal government would give each former slave family "forty acres and a mule" proved to be just that. A small amount of abandoned and confiscated land was turned over to Negroes, but most of the small appropriations for aiding the former slaves were devoted to general relief or educational purposes.

By failing to do more to develop the economic self-sufficiency of the former slaves, the victorious North laid the groundwork for the creation of a sharecropping system that offered Negroes little more opportunity than the antebellum plantation system. After a brief period of disorganization and freedom, the former slaves returned to the land to be employed as day workers or to become sharecroppers. Even in the absence of land reform, the situation of the former slaves would have been much improved by an enlightened legal regulation of the tenancy system. There were a great number of state laws designed to defend the planters' interests. There were virtually none which protected the interests of the tenants. The tenant had no right to permanency of tenure, he seldom had any right to reimbursement for permanent improvements to the land, and he had no redress in his contractual rights. These "tenancy" laws worked to the disadvantage of poor whites as well as Negroes and are part of the explanation for the great extent of white poverty in the South today. Still the system worked most strongly against the Negro.

Black Codes and Jim Crow

Embittered by their loss to the North during the Civil War, Southern whites moved at the first opportunity to emasculate the freedom of their former slaves. The states of the Confederacy signaled their intentions in this respect almost immediately. In the period following the Civil War (1865–67) and before Reconstruction, eight Southern States passed Black Codes which seriously limited the freedom of the Negro population. The apprenticeship, vagrancy, and similar provisions of these statutes forced Negroes into situations where they were under the uncontrolled supervision of their former masters or other white men. In many cases the Negro was free in name only. These Black Codes enraged the North and added fuel to the demand for more drastic Reconstruction measures. During the period of "Radical Reconstruction" these laws were abolished, but soon after the federal presence left the South with the Compromise of 1877, not to return for three generations, the codes reappeared in only slightly modified forms.

As a result of the Civil War and Reconstruction amendments, Negro men were given the right to vote in the whole Union. In the North this change became permanent. In the South the right was soon abridged. This difference is of considerable importance in explaining the greater tendency of the South to use the law to enforce segregation and discrimination. In the first instance, Southerners relied principally on violence and intimidation, symbolized by the Klu Klux Klan, to disenfranchise the freedman. However, with the overthrow of the Reconstruction governments in all Southern states, an intricate body of election laws replaced violence and threats of violence as the principal means of controlling and finally abolishing the Negro vote.

In 1883 the Supreme Court declared the Civil Rights Bill of 1875 unconstitutional insofar as it referred to acts of social discrimination by individuals. This ruling provided the opening wedge for the Jim Crow legislation of the Southern states and municipalities. Since the Reconstruction amendments to the Constitution remained in force, it was necessary to create the legal fiction of "separate but equal." "Separate but equal" became the shield behind which Southern states and municipalities developed the system of separate and outrageously unequal education and other public services that must share a major portion of the responsibility for the continued low levels of Negro income and opportunities.

The Journey to the "Promised Land"

Internal migration of Negroes within the United States in the period since the Civil War must be numbered among the more significant factors in improving the economic position of the Negro. Prior to the Civil War the migration of Negroes to the North was limited. Slavery was illegal outside the South, and thus the move-

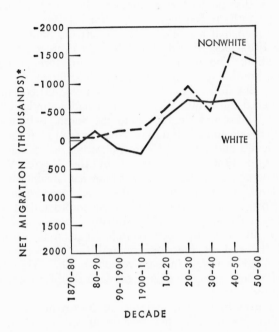

* Net outmigration from the South is negative

Source: U.S. Bureau of the Census, *Statistical Abstract of the United States: 1965* (86th Ed.), Table No. 23 and 33; and Hope T. Eldridge and Dorothy S. Thomas, *Population Redistribution and Economic Growth, United States, 1870–1950*, Vol. III, *Demographic Analysis and Interrelations* (Philadelphia, Pa.: The American Philosophical Society, 1964).

Figure 2. *White and Nonwhite Net Migration from the South by Decade, 1870–1960.*

ment was confined to the small population of free Negroes and runaways. With emancipation, limitations on the mobility of the Negro population were abolished and a more substantial movement began. As illustrated in Figure 2, during the first full decade following the Civil War an estimated 68,000 Negroes (net) left the South. Negro net migration from the South increased in each decade thereafter and had reached nearly 200,000 by the decade 1900–1910.*

The industrial expansion created by World War I and changes in the Southern economy moved Negro migration to Northern cities to a new level. A decline in foreign immigration further increased the demand for Southern Negroes in the North.† As a result of these forces, more than half a million Negroes left the South (net) during the decade 1910–1920. World War I had an even greater impact on white migration. The number of native and foreign born whites entering the South exceeded the number leaving in the decade before the war. But during the decade 1910–1920, 431,000 more whites left than entered the South. World War II had a similar effect on the migration of whites and Negroes from the South. Between 1940 and 1950 more than one and a half million Negroes (net) left the South.

Both the levels and rates of Negro migration reflect the differential pattern of opportunity as perceived by the Negro. While many Southern Negroes may have been somewhat disillusioned by the "promised land," most obtained a substantial increase in income for moving to Northern cities. The extent of this improvement is suggested by some recent earnings data. The statistics summarized in Table 1 illustrate the difference between average Negro male earnings in the South and the rest of the country and the discrepancy between Negro and white earnings in each region in 1960. The stratification by years of school completed is a crude attempt to adjust for differences in productivity.

The differences in median earnings of Negro males in the North and the South exceed $1,200 per year for all six education categories. If the underlying data can be interpreted as reflecting the expected earnings in the North and South of Negroes having a particular level of educational preparation, the average Southern Negro with less than seven years of education could expect to increase his money income by 90 per cent by moving North. The smallest percentage increase is 28 per cent for Southern Negroes with four or more years of college.

The estimates of Negro earnings by education class as a percentage of white earnings in the same region also indicate the greater op-

---

* The definition of the South used in Fig. 2 is more restrictive than that used previously; it omits Delaware, Maryland, and Washington, D.C.

† During the five-year period 1916–1920, foreign immigration to the United States was approximately one and a quarter million. By comparison, it was nearly five million and four and a half million for the previous two half-decades. Following World War I, foreign immigration recovered somewhat, totaling just over two and a half million between 1920 and 1925. Thereafter it never exceeded one and one half million in any five-year period. U.S. Bureau of the Census, *Statistical Abstract of the United States: 1965,* 86th ed. (Washington, D.C.: Government Printing Office, 1965), p. 92.

TABLE 1

Medium Earnings of Males, 25 to 64 Years Old, in the Experienced Civilian Labor Force, by Years of School Completed and Color, 1960

Years of School Completed	Negro Earnings			Negroes Earnings as a Percentage of White	
	North	South	North Minus South	North	South
Elementary					
0 to 7	$3,553	$1,873	$1,680	83%	63%
8 years	3,802	2,437	1,365	80	63
High School					
1 to 3	4,042	2,587	1,455	76	57
4 years	4,397	2,886	1,511	77	55
College					
1 to 3	4,674	3,360	1,314	74	57
4 years or more	5,537	4,308	1,229	70	58
Total, 25 to 65 years old	4,017	2,238	1,779	73	49

Source: U.S. Bureau of the Census, *U.S. Census of Population: 1960, Subject Reports, Occupation by Earnings and Education* (Washington, D.C.: Government Printing Office, 1963), Table 2 and 3.

portunities available to Negroes outside the South. In both regions Negroes earn significantly less than whites of comparable education, but this discrepancy is considerably larger in the South. For example, Negroes with less than seven years of elementary education earn only 83 per cent as much as whites with that much education in the North; but in the South they earn only 63 per cent as much.

Thus, it appears that Negro migrants from the South typically receive a large economic return for migration. This return reflects the combined effects of higher average wages in Northern metropolitan areas and the apparently lesser degree of labor market discrimination found there. The large-scale migration of Negroes from the South to the North and the lower rates of Southern white migration would seem to confirm these statements.

As a result of the massive migrations of the 1940's and 1950's, the metropolitan areas of the North and West became major centers of Negro population. In 1940 these areas accounted for only 20 per cent of all Negroes in the country. Just two decades later 37 per cent of all Negroes lived there. When they reached Northern metropolitan areas, Negro migrants found that their housing choices were sharply limited. The combination of large-scale migration and restrictions on

Negro residential choice led to the rapid growth of central city ghettos in the North.

Some indication of the effect of migration on the growth of Northern ghettos and the population composition of central cities is suggested by the data in Table 2. The contribution of migration to these changes

TABLE 2

Change in White and Nonwhite Central City and Suburban Ring Populations 1950–60 (thousands)

	Central City		Suburban Ring	
	White	Negro	White	Negro
Baltimore	−113	100	324	7
Boston	−130	23	278	3
Chicago	−399	320	1,076	34
Cleveland	−142	103	367	2
Detroit	−363	182	904	19
New York	−476	240	1,777	67
Philadelphia	−225	153	700	38
Pittsburgh	− 91	18	257	7
St. Louis	−168	61	429	18
San Francisco	−148	67	554	25
Washington, D.C.	−173	131	553	18

Source: U.S. Bureau of the Census, *1960 Census of Population, Standard Metropolitan Areas*, PC (3)–1D (Washington, D.C.: Government Printing Office, 1963).

is made even clearer by examining the components of Negro population increase. Net in-migration of Southern Negroes accounted for 54 per cent of the 2.7 million increase in Northern Negro population in the decade 1950–1960. Data on more recent population changes are scanty, but estimates suggest that Negro net in-migration to the North is lower for the period 1960–1966.

CONTEMPORARY FACTORS

The preceding discussion of the historical factors underlying the present economic condition of the Negro American emphasizes the continuity with the past. The current low incomes of the Negro can only be understood in the light of historical circumstances and past discrimination. There is little that well-meaning individuals or even society at large can do about past injustices and lost opportunities, except to recognize their role in disadvantaging today's Negro minority and to perceive in them the justification for special and unusual efforts to overcome the current gap between the economic positions of white and Negro Americans.

Unlike the historical factors, the contemporary causes of Negro low incomes are matters that can be affected by both individuals and society. The discussion begins with an attempt to determine how much of the differences in Negro and white income is attributable to discrimination.

The costs of racial discrimination can be discussed from at least two points of view: the cost to the national economy (the reduction of gross national product) and the cost to the nonwhite minority. Economic losses to the economy as a whole result from the failure to utilize and develop fully the existing and potential skills of the nonwhite population. In 1962 Edward Denison, drawing on figures first developed by Gary Becker, estimated that national income could be increased by 0.8 per cent simply through elimination of the market discrimination against Negroes.[12] Moreover, he concluded that the combined effects of making the work qualifications of Negroes comparable to those of whites and eliminating employment discrimination would increase the national product by something on the order of 4 per cent. Denison further concludes:

> The disadvantages faced by the average Negro child in developing his work potential are, by comparison with those of the average white child, huge. They relate to home and neighborhood environment, schools, and incentives, in a complex and mutually re-enforcing manner. Job discrimination against well-qualified adult Negroes dulls the incentive for the young to prepare themselves for the better jobs.[13]

In 1965 the Council of Economic Advisers published an estimate of the economic cost of discrimination. It stated that the elimination of discrimination in employment would increase the national income by $12.8 billion and that providing Negroes with equivalent education to that of whites would increase national income by an additional $7.8 million. (See the article, "The Economic Cost of Discrimination," pp. 58–59 of this volume.) The combined effects of these adjustments provide an estimated increase in gross national product of 3.7 per cent.

An estimate of the economic cost of discrimination to nonwhites was prepared by Paul M. Siegel (pp. 60–67 of this volume). After correcting for Negro-white differences in education, occupation, and region of residence, Siegel concluded that the cost of being a Negro is roughly $1,000 per year.

Otis Dudley Duncan has made one of the most ambitious attempts to evaluate the effect of historical and contemporary factors on Negro incomes.[14] Using a sample of native men twenty-five to sixty-four years old with nonfarm backgrounds (excluding men whose fathers held farm occupations), Duncan estimated a multiple equation model that sought to explain the number of siblings, the years of education, the occupational status, and the incomes of white and Negro males. The statistical model consisted of a sequence of four equations (one for each of the four variables). The number of brothers and sisters of a white or Negro male is "explained" in terms of his parents' education and occupation (actually the education of either his mother or father, depending on which was determined to be the "head of household"). The number of siblings "explained" by Equation 1 and parents' education and occupation is then used in Equation 2 to explain the respondent's education. Equation 3 explains his occupational status in terms of his parents' education and occupation, the number of siblings in his family, and his education. Finally, in Equation 4 his occupational status and all preceding variables are used to explain his income.

By solving this four-equation model, Duncan obtains estimates of how much of the difference in the incomes of Negro and white males included in his sample is attributable to differences in Negro and white characteristics and how much to discrimination. Duncan determined that differences in the family background account for $1,010, or just over one quarter, of the total gap in white and Negro incomes of $3,790. This combines both the direct and indirect effects on income of belonging to families with a large number of siblings and which are headed by persons with little education and low occupational status.

Duncan then examines the hypothetical consequences of eliminating educational differences between Negro and white males, except those produced by differences in family background that are accounted for in the above calculation. The total education gap between whites and Negroes in the sample is 2.3 years; the difference which cannot be accounted for by the effects of parents' education and occupation and by number of siblings is 1.2 years. This latter educational difference accounts for $520 of the total $3,790 difference in Negro-white incomes, or less than one-seventh.

Roughly half the occupational gap is explained by previously considered differences in family background and education. The remainder, which Duncan tentatively labels "occupational discrimination," is due to the fact that Negroes who are as well educated as whites (in terms of schooling) and from families of comparable size and socioeconomic level do not have access to employment of equal occupational status. "Occupational discrimination" accounts for more than one-fifth of the total dollar gap in Negro-white incomes.

After attributing $830 of the Negro-white income difference to "occupational discrimination," $520 to educational discrimination, and

$1,010 to differences in family background, a sum of $1,430 remains. Commenting on this difference, Duncan concludes:

> This is about three-eighths of the total gap of $3,790. Unless and until we can find other explanations for it, this must stand as an estimate of income discrimination. . . . Specifically, it is the difference between Negro and white incomes that cannot be attributed to differential occupational levels, differential educational attainment . . . , differences in size of family of origin, or differences in the socioeconomic status thereof.[15]

Education

Education has a special importance in discussions of economic opportunity. This importance follows from the consensus that investments in human capital, of which education is the most important, are perhaps the major determinant of earnings. Thus it is not surprising that social scientists have given particular attention to the quantity and quality of education obtained by whites and blacks in their efforts to explain the large discrepancy between white and Negro incomes.

The relationship between Negro education and incomes is complex. On the average the Negroes receive fewer years of education than whites, and those fewer years of schooling are generally lower in quality. Moreover, because of discrimination, Negroes generally receive smaller economic rewards for their education.

Formal schooling is by no means the only type of investment in human capital, but the importance of a minimum amount of formal education cannot be denied. One crude measure of the amount of schooling obtained by Negroes is the per cent of persons twenty-five years and over who have completed less than five years of school. Five years of good schooling would appear to be close to the minimum level of educational preparation needed to perform most tasks in an industrialized society. In 1960 only 7 per cent of whites, but 24 per cent of Negroes, failed to meet this minimum standard.[16] In the Deep South, 39 per cent of all nonwhites over twenty-five years of age had completed fewer than five years of school.* These differences would appear to provide part of the "explanation" for the lower incomes of Negroes.

The substantial differences in the years of school completed are only part of the story. Available data indicate that education received in Negro, and particularly Southern Negro, schools is markedly inferior to that obtained in predominantly white schools. The inadequacy of Negro education in Southern schools first became widely

* The Deep South includes South Carolina, Georgia, Alabama, Mississippi, Arkansas, and Louisiana.

recognized during World War II as a result of the nation's experience with the Selective Service System. For the entire United States approximately forty out of every one thousand registrants were rejected as deficient on the basis of a standardized written test.[17] Rejection rates for Negroes, particularly for Southern Negroes, were much higher. The rejection rate was 25 per one thousand for all whites and 49 per one thousand for Southern whites. The rejection rate for Negroes was 50 per one thousand for Northern and Western states and 180 per one thousand for Southern states.

Prior to 1954 when the Supreme Court declared school segregation unconstitutional, seventeen states and the District of Columbia maintained separate schools systems.[18] Thus reasonably accurate information on per pupil expenditures for Negro and white elementary schools is available before 1954. In 1951–52, current expenditures in Mississippi's white schools were $147 per pupil per year; in its Negro schools they were $32 per pupil. Comparable statistics for other Southern states in the same year were $138 and $77 in Arkansas, $172 and $108 in Alabama, $196 and $98 in South Carolina, and $221 and $160 in Florida. Figures for earlier years were similar.[19]

Even larger differentials appear to have existed earlier in the century. A study published in 1917 provides crude estimates of public expenditures per capita for Negroes and whites during the period immediately preceding World War I.[20] These statistics were obtained by dividing total salaries for teachers in Negro and white schools by the number of Negro and white children between the ages of six and fourteen. As smaller proportions of Negro children were in school, this exaggerates somewhat the discrepancy between the white and Negro per pupil expenditures for those students actually in school. The study determined that school expenditures in the Southern states as a whole were $10.32 for each white and $2.89 for each Negro child annually.

When counties were classified according to their proportion of Negroes, the inequality increased as the proportion of Negroes to total population increased. Expenditures per capita were roughly the same in counties having less than 10 per cent Negro population— $7.96 per capita for Negroes and $7.23 per capita for whites; they were most dissimilar in counties with over 75 per cent Negroes— $22.22 per capita for whites and $1.78 per capita for Negroes.

These results, surprising even for the early period under discussion, are attributable to the then prevalent method of allocating state education funds among counties. Funds were allocated on the basis of total population without regard to race. Thus, a large Negro population was as much of an asset to a county school system as a large white population. Funds were divided between the races by the county board of education and supplemented by local taxes voted by the county. Accordingly, appropriations for Negro schools were almost entirely dependent on the local sentiment of the white school board.

Per pupil expenditures in Negro schools were considerably higher in the border states than in the Deep South. This was partly explained by the relative sparseness of the Negro population and the high cost of providing many small Negro schools. It is also partly explained by the fact that a larger proportion of Negro students attended high school in the border states. Even so, there is a striking parallelism between the Negro right to vote in the border states and the better school facilities provided.

The well-known, if controversial, study, *Equality of Educational Opportunity*, popularly referred to as the Coleman Report, provides more recent confirmation of the low levels of Negro educational achievement.[21] On the basis of a large-scale national survey, the report concluded that twelfth grade Negro students in the metropolitan South had an average verbal ability 4.2 grades below white students in the metropolitan Northeast. The discrepancy was even larger in the nonmetropolitan South, where they lagged 5.2 grades behind. Southern whites also lagged behind whites attending school in the Northeast, but the gap was much smaller than for Southern Negroes. In the metropolitan South the average white twelfth grader was less than one year (0.9) behind twelfth grade white students in the Northeast. For the nonmetropolitan South the gap was 1.5 years.

While the Coleman Report's findings indicate that both Southern whites and Negroes test somewhat below their counterparts in other parts of the country, the most striking finding is the low level of Negro educational achievement in all regions. Twelfth grade Negroes in the metropolitan Northeast and Midwest average 3.3 grades behind twelfth grade whites in verbal ability. True, this is nearly a grade better than the performance of Negroes in the metropolitan South, who average 4.2 grades behind twelfth grade whites attending school in the Northeast, and nearly two grades better than Negroes in the nonmetropolitan South, who average 5.2 grades behind twelfth grade whites attending school in the Northeast. Still, it is hardly a record about which the North can brag.

LABOR MARKET DISCRIMINATION

Labor market discrimination assumes a wide variety of forms. Negroes are barred altogether from some firms and industries. In other circumstances firms hire Negroes, but only for low skilled, low paying jobs and refuse to promote them. Other firms, while perhaps not consciously following discriminatory practices, restrict their recruiting to sources and methods that limit the number of Negro applicants. Still others sign labor agreements with discriminating unions. In many of these and other instances, Negroes are barred from training and apprenticeship programs that are prerequisite to certain trades, occupations, or skilled jobs.

The locus of discrimination within the firm or union varies widely and frequently is difficult to determine. Top management of a large company may imagine it is pursuing an equal opportunity policy. However, company policy is often of no avail when personnel managers, foremen, or other middle and lower management personnel continue to discriminate against minorities in recruitment, employment, and promotion. It has been suggested, with only a little bit of humor, that the most effective policy for combating racial discrimination in employment might be to require that 10 per cent of all personnel men be black.

Discrimination in employment exists in all parts of the country. However, the discriminatory practices prevalent in Southern labor markets deserve special mention. In the South, Negroes are often excluded from particular occupations, restricted to segregated units within an establishment, and limited to separate Negro seniority and promotion lines. Until very recently such policies were quite explicit and were frequently defended by management and labor leaders as necessary or even desirable. With the growing array of federal civil rights legislation and the greater militancy of Southern Negroes, firms and unions have become less open about these actions. Herbert Hill, National Labor Director of the NAACP, provides an excellent summary of these discriminatory employment practices in Southern industry (pp. 78–88 of this volume).

Outside the South, management and labor leaders almost always deny the existence of employment discrimination. Even so the less overt practices common in the remainder of the country can be almost as effective in excluding Negroes from jobs as the more visible practices found in the South. Ironically, because of their more explicit character, it may be possible to force a more rapid elimination of discriminatory practices in Southern than in Northern labor markets.

Evidence that discriminatory practices are commonplace in the North is provided by several studies cited in Paul Norgren and Samuel Hill, *Toward Fair Employment*.[22] A 1953 study of employment practices of 1,200 Pennsylvania firms concluded that nine-tenths of the surveyed firms practiced some degree of discrimination in hiring, apprenticing, and promoting workers. A 1958 report on employment practices in Ohio reached similar conclusions. At the time of these studies neither state had an enforceable Fair Employment Practices law. The subsequent enactment of such laws has unquestionably produced improvement, but employment discrimination is still widespread.

Labor unions have come under intense criticism in recent years for

their role in limiting nonwhite employment opportunities. The na-
tional federations (the AFL, the CIO, and the AFL-CIO) have al-
ways endorsed the principle that there should be no barriers to Negro
membership.[23] The dominant national labor organization in the period
1886–1935 was the AFL (American Federation of Labor). Samuel
Gompers, its first president, and other leaders were committed to
organizing workers without regard to race or religion. This policy was
maintained until about 1895, when the machinists were admitted to
the Federation; they agreed to remove their race bar from their con-
stitution but simply shifted it to their ritual. Ideologically, the AFL
never abandoned its opposition to excluding Negroes from its af-
filiated unions, but its leadership eventually accepted the reality of
racial discrimination among its locals and decided it was better to
organize whites and Negroes into segregated locals than not to or-
ganize them at all. After 1900, the Federation admitted many unions
whose constitutions barred Negroes from membership and permitted
some affiliates to change their constitutions to accomplish this purpose.
    In 1935 the CIO (Committee of Industrial Organizations) was es-
tablished within the AFL. Three years later, when the member unions
were expelled, they reconstituted themselves as the Congress of In-
dustrial Organizations. The CIO adopted an aggressive equalitarian
position from its inception. One reason was its emphasis on organiz-
ing mass production industries employing large numbers of Negroes.
Another was the ideological positions held by many of its leaders.
Finally, the structure of the industries the CIO was trying to penetrate
gave it little choice. Because they do not control jobs, industrial unions,
unlike craft unions that dominated the AFL, have very little con-
trol over the racial composition of their membership. They merely
attempt to organize workers who are already employed. Thus they
have far less opportunity for discrimination than craft unions, which
often control the supply of labor.
    These different attitudes and realities of the CIO and AFL toward
equality are reflected in statistics on union membership by Negroes.
In 1945 the CIO had approximately 400,000 Negro members, or 6.7
per cent of its total membership. In the same year the AFL had about
300,000 Negro members, many in segregated locals, or about 3.4 per
cent of its total membership. This latter statistic represented a sig-
nificant increase, resulting in large part from CIO competition. In
1926–1928 Negroes accounted for about 2.8 per cent of the AFL's
membership.[24]
    The national and local unions of the AFL and CIO have great
autonomy, and the antidiscriminatory posture of the federations were
often in conflict with practices of their national and local unions. This
was particularly true of the AFL. In 1930 a minimum of twenty-six
national unions barred Negroes from membership by formal means.

By 1943, the number of restrictive unions had been reduced to about fourteen, including seven of which were AFL affiliates; by 1949 the number had been reduced to nine, only one of which was a member of the AFL. The last AFL-CIO affiliates to remove their race bars were the formerly independent railway trainmen and locomotive firemen, who dropped these provisions from their constitutions in 1960 and 1963 respectively.

The importance of this decline in formal barriers to Negro membership is easily exaggerated. Many local affiliates of these international unions, as well as others which never had had any formal prohibition, continue to exclude Negroes by informal means.

Barriers to entry into apprenticeship programs have been the principal means of excluding Negroes from these skilled trades. The 1960 Census reported that there were only 2,191 nonwhite apprentices in the country, or 2.5 per cent of the total, which admittedly is an improvement over the 1.9 per cent figure for 1950. The paucity of Negro apprentices in specific trades and cities has been confirmed in numerous studies.[25] The underrepresentation of Negroes both in these skilled trades and in their apprenticeship programs cannot be questioned. However, the reasons for this underrepresentation include more than simply racial discrimination. Many craftsmen strongly believe that they possess a kind of "property right" over their crafts and unions, that they have the right to determine who should enter the trade, and that it is only fair for their sons, nephews, other close relations, and the sons of close friends to have first chance. Few of these are Negroes. They are inclined to resist the entry of any strangers into the craft, and Negroes often may be simply the most visible of these.

Even when they do not discriminate actively, unions can insure there will be few Negro members and apprentices simply by remaining passive. Lack of knowledge and the separation between union halls and the ghetto typically will insure few Negro applicants. These problems of information and accessibility are not limited to apprenticeship and training programs and may partially explain the high unemployment rates and low incomes of Negroes. The employment access problem, as it has become known, illustrates the manner in which the various kinds of discrimination reinforce one another. Housing market discrimination confines Negroes to a few centrally located neighborhoods. Suburbanization of employment during the postwar period has increased distance between these centrally located neighborhoods and many employment centers. Negroes seeking employment at these distant suburban workplaces must be prepared to spend a great deal of time and money commuting to and from what is often a low-wage job; many are discouraged. Housing discrimination may in this way reduce Negro employment and incomes.[26] The extent and causes of housing market segregation are the subjects of the next section.

DISCRIMINATION IN HOUSING

Residential segregation in urban areas has existed for several decades. The "massive" central city ghettos in the North provide the "classic" model. In older Southern cities the central ghetto is often less dominant, and several smaller Negro residential areas often replace the "massive" central ghetto found in Northern cities. This pattern is a vestige of an earlier period, when residential segregation was not needed to enforce social segregation and when accessibility to the Negro (servant) population was valued by the white population. In addition to these scattered Negro neighborhoods in the city, there were sizable Negro farm populations and even communities at the periphery. Today these former agriculture settlements have become surrounded by suburban development and reduce further the spatial concentration of the Negro population. Of course, this source of "suburban" (rural) Negro population is almost entirely absent in the North because Negroes were never a very important part of the agricultural labor force. With increased pressure by civil rights groups for integration in schools, restaurants, and other aspects of urban life, Southern metropolitan areas appear to be moving rapidly toward emulating the "classic" ghetto model of Northern cities.

Negroes in Cities by Karl and Alma Taeuber contains the most comprehensive description of residential segregation in American cities.[27] Relying primarily on census statistics for city blocks, the Taeubers calculated segregation indexes for a large number of American cities in 1940, 1950, and 1960. These segregation indexes assume values between zero and one hundred. A value of zero indicates a completely even distribution of Negroes, i.e., every block has the same proportion of Negroes. A value of one hundred indicates the opposite situation of a completely uneven or segregated distribution, i.e., each block contains only whites or Negroes, but not both. The higher the value of the index, the higher the degree of residential segregation, and conversely the lower the value, the lesser the degree of residential segregation. The actual value of the index indicates the proportion of Negroes that would have to move to predominantly or exclusively white blocks if a particular city were to achieve an unsegregated pattern of residence.

The values for 207 American cities in 1960 ranged from 60.4 in San Jose, California, to 98.1 in Fort Lauderdale, Florida. Half of the cities had segregation indexes above 87.8, and only eight cities had values below 70. Thus, in all but eight of the 207 cities for which indexes were computed, at least 70 per cent of the Negroes would have to move to formerly all white blocks to remove all vestiges of discrimination. In half the cities nearly nine out of every ten families would have to move to white neighborhoods.[28] No elaborate analysis is needed to conclude from these figures that a high degree of residential segregation of Negroes is a general characteristic of American cities.

Another important dimension of housing market segregation is the token representation of Negroes in suburban areas. There is more than a germ of truth in the characterization of the increasingly black central city being strangled by a noose of white suburbs. In 1960 the 216 metropolitan areas of the United States were 11 per cent Negro. However, 17 per cent of the central city populations were Negro as contrasted with only 5 per cent of the suburban populations. If Southern metropolitan areas, with their suburban (agriculture) Negro population, are omitted, the underrepresentation of Negroes in the suburbs becomes even more apparent. In 1960 Negroes comprised over 15 per cent of the population of central cities outside the South, but less than 3 per cent of their suburban populations.

Socioeconomic Determinants of Segregation

Numerous explanations have been offered for the segregation of central city housing markets and the virtual exclusion of Negroes from the rapidly growing suburbs. One of the most common is the contention that Negroes are concentrated within particular portions of central cities because they are poor, spend too little on housing, or differ systematically from the majority white population in characteristics that affect their choice of residence. It is relatively easy to devise quantitative measures of such frequently mentioned socioeconomic variables as family income, education, occupation, housing expenditures, rental outlays, and the value of owner-occupied dwelling units.

Without exception tests of the socioeconomic explanation of housing market segregation have determined that only a fraction of the observed pattern of Negro residential segregation can be explained by low incomes or other measurable systematic differences in the characteristics of Negroes and whites. Despite this evidence, the myth still is widely accepted even among those who generally support the goal of racial integration.

A variety of empirical methods have been used to test this hypothesis. One of the simplest is illustrated by Table 3. These data refute the view that the concentration of Negroes in central cities and their low penetration of suburban areas is attributable to their low incomes. If low income explains the concentration of Negroes in central cities, it also should be true that few low income whites live in suburban areas and that most of the small Negro middle class should

TABLE 3

Per Cent of White and Negro Families Living in the Suburban Ring of the Ten Largest Urbanized Areas, by Income, 1960 *

Urbanized Area	White			Negro		
	All Families	Under $3,000	Over $10,000	All Families	Under $3,000	Over $10,000
1. New York	27.8%	16.3%	39.2%	9.4%	8.2%	13.9%
2. Los Angeles– Long Beach	59.5	53.5	57.7	25.1	20.7	28.5
3. Chicago	47.6	37.2	54.7	7.7	5.9	9.0
4. Philadelphia– Camden	47.7	32.7	42.2	11.5	10.1	13.8
5. Detroit	58.9	44.9	63.3	12.1	11.3	12.6
6. San Francisco– Oakland	57.8	48.8	60.8	29.2	25.8	31.5
7. Boston	74.3	64.0	82.4	19.2	13.9	37.7
8. Washington	75.7	59.6	77.3	9.8	10.4	8.4
9. Pittsburgh	70.5	63.3	73.6	29.4	27.1	29.4
10. Cleveland	59.2	39.3	75.2	3.1	2.4	4.3

* For New York and Chicago the suburban ring is the difference between the SMSA and the urban place (central city). For all other cities it is the difference between the urbanized area and central city. San Francisco–Oakland, Los Angeles–Long Beach, and Philadelphia–Camden are counted as two central cities.

Source: U.S. Bureau of the Census, *U.S. Census of Population: 1960.* Vol. I, *Characteristics of the Population.* Parts 6, 10, 15, 23, 24, 32, 34, 37, and 40. Chapter C, General Social and Economic Characteristics, Tables 76 and 78.

live there. Yet, as the data in Table 3 indicate, almost as many low income whites live in the suburban rings of the largest metropolitan areas as live in the central cities, and relatively few high income Negroes reside in suburban areas.

Self-Segregation: A Historical Perspective

Another "explanation" of residential segregation is that the segregation of Negroes is "normal" and should be valued as part of the diversity of a pluralistic society rather than deplored. Proponents of this view point to the immigrant colonies that are evident even today in many cities as evidence of the "normality" of this behavior. It is true that a number of identifiable groups have exhibited some degree of segregation in American cities, but the differences between their experience and that of the American Negro are such as to invalidate the historical analogy.

Numerous comparative studies of the residential segregation of Negroes and other racial, religious, and ethnic groups in American cities all reach nearly identical conclusions. The degree of residential segregation of Negroes is greater than that exhibited by any other identifiable subgroup in American history. Segregation of other groups has declined over time, while that of Negroes has remained at a high level, and possibly increased. Such studies do not disprove conclusively the hypothesis of self-segregation, but they make the argument less plausible. To accept self-segregation as a significant explanation of Negro residential segregation, one must assume that Negroes have much stronger ties to their community than other groups. Comparative analyses by Karl and Alma Taeuber of Chicago Negroes and other residentially segregated groups (pp. 100–111 of this volume) and the studies by Stanley Lieberson are of particular interest in this respect.

Imposed Segregation and Self-Segregation

It is virtually impossible to evaluate the role of self-segregation as long as strong traces of community (white) antagonism toward Negro efforts to leave the ghetto remain. Perhaps the unwillingness of a Negro to risk his life and those of his family by attempting to move into a white neighborhood should be regarded as self-segregation, but this is hardly what most persons who hold this view have in mind. The physical dangers of moving out of the ghetto probably are less today than in the past, but many subtle and indirect forms of intimidation and discouragement still exist.

Self-segregation must refer to a completely voluntary decision to remain in a total or predominantly Negro neighborhood, not a largely involuntary need to remain. Obviously the distinction is a difficult one to make since it is made in the mind of each individual. Negroes may have exaggerated views of the difficulty of finding appropriate accommodations in white neighborhoods and of the hostility they will encounter among their new neighbors. Still there are enough accounts and other evidence of the obstacles Negroes encounter to make a strong *prima facie* case of involuntary segregation for the researcher and more importantly for the isolated Negro considering a move out of the ghetto.

Evidence regarding the methods used to enforce housing market segregation is somewhat more difficult to obtain today than in the past. A decline in clear-cut community approval for such practices and an increasing number of open occupancy laws, which forbid discrimination in the sale and rental of housing on the basis of race, have caused opponents of open housing to resort to more subtle and secretive methods. This is a new situation. Until very recently the most important devices used to enforce segregation could hardly be called subtle. Knowledge of these earlier methods of maintaining segregation is important because residential patterns have a great deal of inertia. Even if there were no resistance to Negro occupancy outside the ghetto in the future, the cumulative effects of decades of discriminatory practices will have long-lasting impacts. If these inimical patterns of housing market segregation are to be destroyed, strong laws, vigorous enforcement, and powerful incentives for integration will be necessary. In determining the range of corrective action both needed and justified, it is important to recognize the extent of discriminatory actions and particularly the complicity of government and law.

Racial zoning was one of the earliest methods used to confine Negroes to particular neighborhoods. The Louisville ordinance, the first example of racial zoning, became a kind of a model statute and was widely copied. It provided simply that any block containing a majority of white people should be designated a white residence block, and any block containing a majority of Negroes should be designated a Negro residence block, and that no Negroes could move into white residence blocks and vice versa. Racial zoning was so unsubtle and so patently unconstitutional that it was invalidated by the U.S. Supreme Court in 1913 as a violation of the fourteenth amendment. Even so racial zoning existed in Birmingham, Alabama as late as 1950.[29]

Enforcement of residential segregation by public officials was not limited to Birmingham or to the South. For example, Morton Grodzins in 1958 quoted a builder on the attitudes and behavior of Philadelphia officials:

A Philadelphia builder recently told an interviewer that he would very much like to sell suburban houses to Negroes, but that it was impossible because it would ruin him economically. "If I sold just one suburban home to a Negro the local building inspectors would have me moving pipes three-eighths of an inch every afternoon in every one of the places I was building; and moving a pipe three-eighths of an inch is mighty expensive if you have to do it in concrete." [30]

The most important devices for maintaining racial segregation were deed restrictions. Race restrictive covenants came into widespread use during the 1920's when they were promoted by property owner associations, real estate boards, and even by the Federal Housing Association (FHA). Although the courts had invalidated racial zoning ordinances, for many years they regarded racial covenants as a purely private matter. In 1947 the Supreme Court ruled that the enforcement of racial covenants by the courts was illegal. By that time the damage had already been done. Most housing sold to whites in the three previous decades was covered by these covenants. Race restrictive covenants remained an effective tool in barring Negroes from white residential areas even after the Supreme Court decision. Many home-owners were unaware that they were no longer legally binding. Others felt they had a moral obligation to honor the agreements, even if they were no longer enforcible in the courts.

Although the actions of the Supreme Court did not eliminate dis-crimination, they were important in removing the sanction of law from these practices. Increasingly those wishing to keep Negroes out of white neighborhoods were forced to rely on "gentlemen's agreements," the action of real estate agents, financial institutions, property owners, and other extralegal or even illegal devices. (See the article by Jack Rothman, pp. 122–27 in this volume.) Even so, these barriers were sufficient to discourage all but the most determined Negroes from attempting to enter a white neighborhood.

In spite of considerable evidence, many people appear to remain un-convinced of the importance of discriminatory practices, particularly the collusive behavior of mortgage lenders, real estate agents, and builders in explaining Negro residential segregation. It must be ad-mitted that much of the evidence of discriminatory practices is almost anecdotal in character. For the social scientist who likes his numbers hard, the evidence on the discriminatory behavior in the real estate market has a disconcerting softness.

The preceding discussion illustrates the difficulty of decomposing the residual that remains after allowing for maximum influence of socio-economic factors. The evaluation of this unexplained residual, which must be due to self-segregation or imposed segregation, is com-plicated by strong interactions that must exist between the two causes. Indeed it is difficult to see how a satisfactory evaluation of the self-segregation hypothesis is possible as long as Negroes believe that sig-nificant white opposition to their moving into white neighborhoods exists.

In evaluating the evidence of discriminatory practices in the housing market, one should not lose sight of the fact that what Negroes believe and feel about restrictions on their residential choices may be even more important than actual circumstances. Thus knowledge of the attitudes and motivations of Negroes is needed in order to evaluate adequately the self-segregation hypothesis, to understand and inter-pret existing patterns of segregation, and to make projections about the future patterns of Negro residence. But obtaining accurate, truth-ful, and meaningful data on attitudes is no simple matter, even under ideal circumstances. These difficulties are compounded for politically sensitive and highly publicized areas such as race. There is a danger that individuals will tell the interviewer what he believes the interviewer wants to hear, what he believes is the generally accepted view, or what is most advantageous for his interests rather than his true attitudes and beliefs. Recognizing these difficulties, surveys such as those reported by William Brink and Louis Harris are almost the only evidence about Negro attitudes available. (See pp. 139–45 of this volume.) They give little support to the self-segregation hypothesis.

CHOICE OF PUBLIC POLICIES

A plethora of public policies have been proposed to improve the economic condition of the Negro, to increase his opportunities, and to combat discrimination. Most programs directed toward improving the current economic condition of the Negro are part of a broader range of antipoverty measures. The incomes and consumption of millions of Negro families would be increased by higher welfare payments and broadened eligibility; several proposed income maintenance programs, such as the negative income tax and family allowances; low income housing programs; and various employment and manpower training programs designed to increase the earnings of the poor. Insofar as an adequate income is essential to enabling families to invest in their children's education and other forms of human capital, these programs can make a major contribution to improving the opportunities and earnings of future generations of Negroes. Negro unrest, by drawing attention to the plight of the poor, may have been a major force behind the war on poverty and may even have caused some refocusing of poverty programs on the Negro population. Still these programs are aimed specifically at the Negro only in the sense that a disproportionate number of Negroes are poor. Moreover, it is well to keep in mind that Negroes are a minority of the poor.

There is increasing agreement that what the poor lack most of all is money and that the emphasis in welfare programs should be shifted from the provision of services to the provision of income. However, there is considerable disagreement about the desirability of income transfers for "able-bodied males." Many persons argue strongly that such transfers would discourage work and suggest instead that government should guarantee employment. The "employer of last resort" proposal is a program of this kind. Proponents of heavier reliance on direct income transfers counter with the arguments that employment guarantee programs would be more expensive than direct payments and that income transfers can be designed to produce strong work incentives. They contend that a measure such as the negative income tax would be much cheaper, would provide a minimum income floor for all groups, and would improve work incentives. Virtually all these proposals are included among the recommendations of the Kerner Commission (pp. 146–52).

A somewhat different set of priorities has been suggested by Daniel Patrick Moynihan, the first executive secretary of the President's Council for Urban Affairs. Moynihan argues that job creation for unemployed blacks should have the highest priority, closely followed by a program of children's allowances. This strategy for combating poverty, and more specifically for improving the economic condition of Negroes, comes directly from his analysis of the Negro family (see pp. 38–44). The controversial Department of Labor report, *The Negro Family: the Case for National Action,* prepared under Moynihan's direction, provides the analytical basis for these recommendations by identifying the deterioration of the Negro family as the major source of the disadvantages experienced by the Negro American. High levels of unemployment among Negro males bear a major portion of the responsibility for the weakness of the Negro family. Moynihan sees programs that guarantee employment for Negro males as the crucial first step in strengthening the Negro family and thereby narrowing the gap in income between Negro and white families.

Programs designed to increase Negro opportunities and antidiscrimination programs have a great deal of overlap, since a lowering of barriers in employment, education, housing, and other fields will widen opportunities. However, there are numerous compensatory measures that seek to increase opportunities without directly attacking discrimination. These include various education, manpower training, and other human capital programs that increase the abilities and skills of Negro workers and thereby permit them to obtain better jobs and increase their incomes, even in the face of continued discrimination. Obviously, such programs are highly complementary with antidiscrimination programs since the increase in incomes produced by better qualifications is influenced strongly by the extent of labor market discrimination.

In the South, the most serious form of discrimination at the end of World War II was denial of the right to vote. It is no accident that the earliest, and probably the most successful, broadly based civil rights activities were concerned with registering Southern Negroes to vote. The ballot is crucial to obtaining positive public action for improving the position of the Negro. While no limitations on the Negro franchise still exist in the South, the change in the region's political climate in the last decade and a half is immense. Negro registration and voting is continuing to increase, and this is causing marked changes in Southern politics and the position of the Negro.

Most antidiscrimination efforts have focused on employment, jobs, housing, and education. Employment discrimination remains pervasive in all regions of the country, but there is some indication that it is slowly giving way before the assault of equal employment opportunity legislation, government contract compliance regulations, moral suasion, and direct action by blacks. The improvement in this area is probably greatest in the North and West, but profound changes are occurring in the employment practices of Southern industry as well.

The Supreme Court decision outlawing school segregation by race had important implications for Negroes living in the South. Although Southern state governments have fought bitterly against school desegregation, there is at least token desegregation almost everywhere. Moreover, under the continual pressure of federal administrators, who are required by law to withhold federal funds from school districts not in compliance with federal desegregation guidelines, school desegregation has begun to be more than tokenism in some parts of the South, especially the border states.

In the North, housing market desegregation is the key to school desegregation. Unfortunately, progress in the area of housing desegregation is less evident than in the area of employment discrimination. But information about changes in racial occupancy is inferior even to that about the labor market, and progress in this crucial area may be more rapid than anyone imagines. Even if 1970 census data reveal more desegregation than anticipated, central city ghettos are continuing to grow in size and population. This is very serious because housing segregation limits Negro opportunities in many subtle and indirect ways. For example, there is growing concern and some evidence that limitations on Negro residential choice may limit Negro employment opportunities and thereby share the responsibility for higher Negro unemployment rates and lower incomes. Similarly, as Chester Rapkin points out there is reason to believe that Negroes are forced to spend more to obtain housing of equal quality as a result of housing market discrimination (see pp. 112–121).

The goals of desegregation and integration have come increasingly under attack since the middle of the 1960's. In part, this is the result of growing doubts about whether the promises of integration will be kept. Increasing numbers of both blacks and whites have become enamored with slogans such as black power, black capitalism, and with notions of economic development of the ghetto. All of these proposals are characterized by an emphasis on improving the Negroes' economic position within the framework of a segregated society. Frances Fox Piven and Richard Cloward, for example, argue that the Negro poor have paid a heavy price for attempts to achieve housing integration (see pp. 175–83). By comparison with many other statements, the position of Piven and Cloward is a limited and pragmatic one. It rests on a political judgment about the relationship between congressional appropriations for low income housing and open housing legislation. Their opinion is that substantially greater appropriations for low income housing programs could be obtained by soft-pedaling integration.

Impatience with the speed of desegregation has spawned a much more ambitious strategy: the economic development of the ghetto. Advocates of this strategy draw a parallel between the ghetto and an underdeveloped nation. Extending this analogy, they propose a policy of economic development for the ghetto. Measures include a variety of subsidies to encourage firms to locate in the ghetto, to foster black owned business in the ghetto, to involve the nonwhite population of the ghetto in the rehabilitation and renewal of its housing stock, and to improve the physical environment of the ghetto. A moderate version of this position argues that regardless of the measures taken to provide housing for Negroes outside the ghetto, the ghetto will continue to exist for decades. Therefore, to improve the condition of the vast majority of Negroes it is essential to renew the ghetto. The Kerner Commission report contains a number of recommendations in this spirit.

A more comprehensive argument for this view is found in a speech by the late Senator Robert F. Kennedy (see pp. 153–63). Senator Kennedy saw ghetto economic development as a necessary precondition to eventual integration of the Negro American into the broader society. In a much quoted campaign speech and a subsequent article prepared for *Nation's Cities,* President Richard M. Nixon outlined his proposal for dealing with the problems of the ghetto: "What we have to do is to get private enterprise into the ghetto, and get the people of the ghetto into private enterprise—not only as workers, but as managers and owners" (see pp. 164–66). The most striking aspect of President Nixon's proposals to aid the nation's slums is their similarity to the legislation proposed by Senator Kennedy.

More extreme views of ghetto development deny that integration is ever possible or desirable and argue for the separate development of black ghettos as an end in itself. John Kain and Joseph Persky present a critique of this strategy (pp. 167–74), and serious questions about the still vaguely defined concept of black capitalism are raised indirectly by Andrew Brimmer (pp. 89–99).

The following selections develop more fully these and many of the questions raised by this essay. The readings are grouped into five broad parts. The first is concerned with the current economic condition of the Negro American and with his progress, both absolute and relative to that of whites in recent decades. Parts 2 and 3 are concerned with the circumstances of the Negro in labor markets and housing markets. The fourth part contains two selections on the attitudes of whites and Negroes toward integration and civil rights. The final part presents a range of alternative proposals for public policy.

NOTES

1. This phrase is used by Claude Brown in *Manchild in the Promised Land* (New York: The MacMillan Company, 1965).
2. U.S. Bureau of the Census, *Current Population Reports*, Series P-60, No. 55, "Family Income Advances, Poverty Reduced in 1967," August 5, 1968, Table 2, p. 4. These estimates are based on a poverty index developed by the Social Security Administration. This index takes into account such factors as family size, number of children, and farm-nonfarm residence. The poverty threshold for a family of four in 1966 and 1967 was $3,335. For nonfarm residents, it ranged from $1,560 for a woman 65 years or older living alone, to $5,440 for a family of seven or more persons.
3. Calculated from U.S. Bureau of the Census, *Statistical Abstract of the United States, 1968* (89th ed.), Table 499, p. 341.
4. 1960 national per capita income figures were reported in *Business International: Weekly Report to Management on Business Abroad* (October 20 and October 27, 1961), pp. 4–5.
5. Charles C. Killingsworth, *Jobs and Income for Negroes* (Ann Arbor, Michigan: Institute of Labor and Industrial Relations, 1968), p. 13.
6. U.S. Bureau of Labor Statistics and U.S. Bureau of the Census, "Social and Economic Conditions of Negroes in the United States" (October 1967), p. 18.
7. *Ibid.*, p. 30.
8. An excellent discussion of the economics of the slave system is found in Alfred Conrad and John R. Meyer, *The Economics of Slavery* (Chicago: Aldine Publishing Company, 1964), Chapter 3. Kenneth M. Stampp, *The Peculiar Institution* (New York: Alfred A. Knopf, 1963) contains a more qualitative description of slavery and its effects on Southern institutions. The period between the Civil War and World War II is critically analyzed in Gunnar Myrdal, *et al.*, *An American Dilemma: The Negro Problem and Modern Democracy* (New York: Harper and Brothers Publishers, 1944).
9. Abner Hurwitz and Carlyle P. Stallings, "Interregional Differentials in Per Capita Real Income Change," in *Regional Income*, Studies in Income and Wealth, 21 (Princeton, N.J.: Princeton University Press, 1957), Table A-9, pp. 260–261.
10. Dale L. Hiestand, *Economic Growth and Employment Opportunities for Minorities* (New York: Columbia University Press, 1964), p. 42.
11. Conrad and Meyer, *op. cit.*
12. Edward F. Denison, *The Sources of Economic Growth in the United States and the Alternatives Before Us* (Washington, D.C.: Committee for Economic Development, 1962), p. 196; and Gary Becker, *The Economics of Discrimination* (Chicago: The University of Chicago Press, 1957), p. 21.
13. Denison, *op. cit.*, p. 197.
14. Otis Dudley Duncan, "Inheritance of Poverty or Inheritance of Race?" in *On Understanding Poverty: Perspectives from the Social Sciences*, ed. Daniel P. Moynihan (New York: Basic Books, 1969).
15. *Ibid.*, p. 40.
16. John F. Kain and Joseph J. Persky, "The North's Stake in Southern Rural Poverty," *Rural Poverty in the United States*, A Report by the President's

National Advisory Commission on Rural Poverty (Washington, D.C.: Government Printing Office, May 1968).

17. Eli Ginzberg and Douglas W. Bray, *The Uneducated* (New York: Columbia University Press, 1953), p. 42.
18. Brown vs. the Board of Education of Topeka, 347 U.S. (1954).
19. Kain and Persky, *op. cit.*, pp. 299–300.
20. U.S. Bureau of Education, *Negro Education*, Bulletin 1916, No. 38 (Washington, D.C.: Government Printing Office, 1917).
21. James S. Coleman, *et al.*, *Equality of Educational Opportunity*, U.S. Office of Education (Washington, D.C.: Government Printing Office, 1966).
22. Paul H. Norgren and Samuel E. Hill, *Toward Fair Employment* (New York: Columbia University Press, 1964).
23. This discussion of labor union practices draws heavily on Ray Marshall, *The Negro Worker* (New York: Random House, 1967), Chaps. 3, 4, and 5; and Marshall, *The Negro and Organized Labor* (New York: John Wiley and Sons, 1965).
24. Marshall, *The Negro Worker*, p. 29.
25. Several of these are cited in Marshall, *The Negro Worker*, p. 65.
26. This question is discussed in John F. Kain, "Housing Segregation, Negro Employment, and Metropolitan Decentralization," *The Quarterly Journal of Economics*, LXXXII, No. 2 (May 1968), 175–197.
27. Karl E. Taeuber and Alma F. Taeuber, *Negroes in Cities: Residential Segregation and Neighborhood Change* (Chicago: The Aldine Publishing Co., 1965).
28. *Ibid.*
29. Robert Thompson, Hylan Lewis, and Davis McEntire, "Atlanta and Birmingham: A Comparative Study in Negro Housing," in *Studies in Housing and Minority Groups*, ed. Nathan Glazer and Davis McEntire (Berkeley & Los Angeles: University of California Press, 1960), p. 59.
30. Morton Grodzins, "The Metropolitan Area as a Racial Problem," in *American Race Relations Today*, ed. Earl Raab (Garden City, N.Y.: Anchor Books, 1962), p. 94. Reprinted from Morton Grodzins, *The Metropolitan Area as a Racial Problem* (Pittsburgh, Pa.: University of Pittsburgh Press, 1958).

PART I

The Economic Condition of the Negro

SOCIAL AND ECONOMIC CONDITIONS OF NEGROES IN THE UNITED STATES

Bureau of Labor Statistics
Bureau of the Census

In the summer of 1967, immediately following the Detroit riots, President Johnson requested the Bureau of Labor Statistics and the Census Bureau "to draw together the latest and most relevant data concerning the social and economic condition of Negroes in America in a simple format that could be easily understood." A statistical report, released by the President in November 1967, showed the changes in income, employment, education, housing, health, and other areas that had occurred in recent years. The introduction of the report summarizes its principal findings.

This is a statistical report about the social and economic condition of the Negro population of the United States. It shows the changes that have taken place during recent years in income, employment, education, housing, health and other major aspects of life. The report was prepared jointly by the Bureau of Labor Statistics and the Bureau of the Census.

Virtually all of the statistics are from the Census or from Federal Government studies designed and conducted by technical experts. Many of the figures have been previously published. Others are scheduled to appear soon in regularly recurring government reports. Some of the data were tabulated specially for this report.

The aim throughout has been to assemble data to be used by government agencies at all levels, and by the general public, to help de-

From Bureau of Labor Statistics and Bureau of the Census, "Social and Economic Conditions of Negroes in the United States," BLS Report No. 332 and Current Population Reports, Series P-23, No. 24 (Washington, D.C.: Government Printing Office, October, 1967).

velop informed judgments on how the Negro is faring in this country.

A statistical report cannot present the complete picture because it is necessarily limited to those aspects of life which can be measured. Many elements which are crucial for a dignified life in a society of equals cannot be measured. Yet much can be learned from a careful examination of the factual evidence at hand.

The statistics provide a mixed picture. There are signs of great improvement in some sections and of deterioration in others. The data show that large numbers of Negroes are for the first time in American history entering into the middle-income bracket and into better environments in which to raise their families.

Yet others remain trapped in the poverty of the slums, their living conditions either unchanged or deteriorating.

The kaleidoscopic pattern begins to make sense only when we stop thinking of the Negro as a homogeneous, undifferentiated group and begin to think of Negroes as individuals who differ widely in their aspirations, abilities, experiences and opportunities.

Millions of Negroes have uprooted themselves in search of better jobs, greater freedom and wider horizons. Many have taken advantage of education and training programs in recent years. The fact that these opportunities exist, and that large numbers of Negroes are using them, proves that there are open avenues of upward mobility in our society. Many who were at the bottom are finding their way up the economic ladder.

The substantial improvement in the national averages for Negroes in income, employment, education, housing and other subjects covered in this report reflect the widespread nature of the social and economic gains experienced by most Negroes in recent years.

Yet, large numbers are living in areas where conditions are growing worse.

In part, the deterioration in the poorest Negro neighborhoods reflects the fact that these areas are constantly losing their most successful people to better neighborhoods, leaving behind the most impoverished. As a first home in the city, these areas also attract rural newcomers who come with the hope—as did immigrants of previous generations—of making a better living, but with few skills to equip them for urban life.

This complicated pattern of progress mixed with some retrogression makes it hazardous to generalize about the social and economic conditions of Negroes in America. The statistics show dramatic achievements; they also reveal a large remaining gap between the circumstances of whites and Negroes.

The single most important fact in the economic life of most Americans—white and Negro alike—is the great productivity of our economy. Millions of Negroes who just a few years ago had small jobs, small incomes and even smaller hopes have made considerable gains. *Although Negro family income remains low in comparison with the rest of the population, the incomes of both whites and Negroes are at an all-time high and during the last year the gap between the two groups has significantly narrowed.*

Still, despite the gains, Negro family income is only 58% of white income. A majority of Negro families still live in the Southern Region where incomes are far below the national average and where employment opportunities for them are more restricted than elsewhere. Outside the South, Negroes do much better. In the Northeast Region —the median family income for Negro families is $5,400—two-thirds the white median; in the North Central area, the median income of Negro families is $5,900—about three-fourths the white median.

Today, over 28% of the nonwhite* families receive more than $7,000 a year—more than double the proportion with incomes that high seven years ago, as measured in constant dollars taking into account changes in prices. Outside the Southern Region, the percentage of Negro families with incomes of $7,000 or more rises to 38%.

The incidence of poverty among nonwhite families remains high, with about one out of three classified as poor. Still, just six years ago one out of two of the nonwhite families were poor. Last year, the number of nonwhites in poverty was reduced by 151,000 families. The majority of nonwhites who are poor work for a living and are not dependent upon welfare assistance.

Whites and Negroes have both benefited from the prosperous conditions of recent years. Continued prosperity for more than six years has brought with it increased job opportunities. Many who had been out of work have moved into jobs; others who worked only part time are now working full time or over time; and still others who were employed at menial tasks have taken advantage of the opportunity for upgrading their skills or status.

Unemployment rates for nonwhites are still twice those of whites, but the level for both groups has dropped dramatically. For nonwhite married men, who are the chief providers in nearly three-fourths of the nonwhite homes, the unemployment rate dropped at a faster rate than for white married men during the last five years and now stands at about 3½%.

Despite the decline in the unemployment rate, nonwhite males are somewhat more likely to be "not in the labor force," that is, neither working nor looking for work.

Further, unemployment has not decreased sharply everywhere. Teen-

* Data for "Negroes" were used where available; in all other cases the data are shown for "nonwhites." Statistics for "nonwhites" generally reflect the condition of Negroes.

age unemployment continues very high at 26%. In one of the worst areas of Cleveland (Hough) unemployment rates from 1960 to 1965 moved downward less than 2 points—and remained at 14% in 1965. The subemployment rate, which reflects part-time work, discouraged workers, and low-paid workers, was 33% in 1966 in the "worst" areas of nine large cities.

The decline in unemployment and the rise in income reflected an expanding range of well-paying jobs. The number of nonwhites in professional, white-collar and skilled jobs went up by nearly half during the past six years.

Even with this substantial progress, it should be noted that Negroes are still far less likely to be in the better jobs. For the first time, however, the numbers of Negroes moving into good jobs has been of sizeable proportions. Since 1960, there has been a net increase of about 250,000 nonwhite professional and managerial workers, 280,000 clerical and sales workers, 190,000 craftsmen, and 160,000 operatives in the steel, automobile, and other durable goods manufacturing industries. There was a net increase of nearly 900,000 nonwhite workers in jobs that tend to have good pay or status during the past six years. Yet, many Negroes remain behind: a nonwhite man is still about three times as likely as a white man to be in a low-paying job as a laborer or service worker.

Education has often been considered as the key to economic success in our society. Recent improvements for nonwhites in this area parallel those previously described in employment and income.

Six years ago, nonwhite young men averaged two years less schooling than white young men. Today the gap is only one-half year. Nonwhite teenage boys are completing high school and going into college in increasing proportions, and for the first time the typical nonwhite young man can be said to be a high school graduate.

Despite the gains in "years of education attained," the only data available that deal with the "level of achievement" show a major gap: Negro students test out at substantially lower levels than white youths; up to 3 years less in the twelfth grade. Further, about 43% of Negro youth are rejected for military service because of "mental" reasons, compared with an 8% rate for white youth.

One of the encouraging signs revealed by this statistical study is the very active participation of Negroes in voting and registration.

Outside of the South, almost as large a proportion of Negro as white adults voted in the 1964 Presidential election. Almost 70% of all registered Negroes voted in the 1966 Congressional election. By 1966 there were over 140 Negroes in State legislatures, almost triple the number four years earlier.

One of the somber notes sounded by this report concerns the increase in residential segregation: a survey of 12 cities in which special censuses have been taken shows increased rates of segregation in eight cities.

But perhaps the most distressing evidence presented in this report indicates that conditions are stagnant or deteriorating in the poorest areas.

About half a million poor Negro families—10% of the total—have lived all their lives in rural areas with very limited opportunities for improvement in education, employment, housing or income.

Another 10%—half a million Negro families—have incomes below the poverty line and live in poor neighborhoods of large central cities. This tenth lives in comparatively wretched conditions—many have poor housing; a sizeable proportion are "broken families"; they are at the bottom of the job ladder; and they have the highest unemployment rates.

The unevenness of social and economic progress among Negroes can be seen most dramatically in the results of the Census that was taken in Cleveland two years ago.

Outside of the poor neighborhoods in Cleveland, Negro families made major gains between 1960 and 1965. Average incomes rose, the incidence of poverty and the number of broken families were reduced.

But in the poorest neighborhoods, all of these social indicators showed decline.

In Hough, which is one of the worst of the poor neighborhoods, the incidence of poverty increased, the proportion of broken homes increased, and the male unemployment rate was virtually unchanged. A similar study was made in various neighborhoods in South Los Angeles after the riot in Watts several years ago, and showed much the same pattern.

Despite the general improvement in the conditions of life for Negroes nationally, conditions have grown worse in places like Hough and Watts. As Negro families succeed, they tend to move out of these economically and socially depressed areas to better neighborhoods where they and their children have the opportunity to lead a better life. They leave behind increasing problems of deprivation in the heart of our largest cities.

The facts in this report thus show a mixture of sound and substantial progress, on the one hand, and large unfulfilled needs on the other. They do not warrant complacency. Neither do they justify pessimism or despair.

THE NEGRO AMERICAN FAMILY
(*The Moynihan Report*)

Office of Policy Planning and Research
United States Department of Labor

The Negro Family, *a 1965 Department of Labor Report, popularly known as the Moynihan report, identifies the family as the basic social unit of American life and argues that the deterioration of the Negro family is the root of the problems of the Negro American. It claims that contrary to the high level of stability maintained by the white family, the family structure of the disadvantaged Negro is chaotic and approaching complete breakdown in many urban areas. The report concludes that a national effort should be made to "strengthen the Negro family."*

At the heart of the deterioration of the fabric of Negro society is the deterioration of the Negro family.

It is the fundamental source of the weakness of the Negro community at the present time.

There is probably no single fact of Negro American life so little understood by whites. The Negro situation is commonly perceived by whites in terms of the visible manifestations of discrimination and poverty, in part because Negro protest is directed against such obstacles, and in part, no doubt, because these are facts which involve the actions and attitudes of the white community as well. It is more difficult, however, for whites to perceive the effect that three centuries of exploitation have had on the fabric of Negro society itself. Here the consequences of the historic injustices done to Negro Americans are silent and hidden from view. But here is where the true injury has occurred: unless this damage is repaired, all the effort to end discrimination and poverty and injustice will come to little.

From "The Negro Family: The Case for National Action," Office of Policy Planning and Research, United States Department of Labor (Washington, D.C.: Government Printing Office, March, 1965).

The role of the family in shaping character and ability is so pervasive as to be easily overlooked. The family is the basic social unit of American life; it is the basic socializing unit. By and large, adult conduct in society is learned as a child.

A fundamental insight of psychoanalytic theory, for example, is that the child learns a way of looking at life in his early years through which all later experience is viewed and which profoundly shapes his adult conduct.

It may be hazarded that the reason family structure does not loom larger in public discussion of social issues is that people tend to assume that the nature of family life is about the same throughout American society.

*   *   *

But there is one truly great discontinuity in family structure in the United States at the present time: that between the white world in general and that of the Negro American.

The white family has achieved a high degree of stability and is maintaining that stability.

By contrast, the family structure of lower class Negroes is highly unstable, and in many urban centers is approaching complete breakdown.

There is considerable evidence that the Negro community is in fact dividing between a stable middle-class group that is steadily growing stronger and more successful, and an increasingly disorganized and disadvantaged lower-class group. There are indications, for example, that the middle-class Negro family puts a higher premium on family stability and the conserving of family resources than does the white middle-class family. . . .

There are two points to be noted in this context.

First, the emergence and increasing visibility of a Negro middle-class may beguile the nation into supposing that the circumstances of the remainder of the Negro community are equally prosperous, whereas just the opposite is true at present, and is likely to continue so.

Second, the lumping of all Negroes together in one statistical measurement very probably conceals the extent of the disorganization among the lower-class group. If conditions are improving for one and deteriorating for the other, the resultant statistical averages might show no change. Further, the statistics on the Negro family and most other subjects treated in this paper refer only to a specific point in time. They are a vertical measure of the situation at a given moment. They do not measure the experience of individuals over time. Thus the average monthly unemployment rate for Negro males for 1964 is recorded as 9 per cent. But *during* 1964, some 29 per cent of Negro males were unemployed at one time or another. Similarly, for example, if 36 per cent of Negro children are living in broken homes *at any specific moment,* it is likely that a far higher proportion of Negro children find themselves in that situation *at one time or another* in their lives.

Nearly a Quarter of Urban Negro Marriages Are Dissolved

Nearly a quarter of Negro women living in cities who have ever married are divorced, separated, or are living apart from their husbands.

The rates are highest in the urban Northeast where 26 per cent of Negro women ever married are either divorced, separated, or have their husbands absent.

*   *   *

Among ever-married nonwhite women in the nation, the proportion with husbands present *declined* in *every* age group over the decade 1950–60, as follows:

Age	Per cent with Husbands Present	
	1950	1960
15–19 years	77.8	72.5
20–24 years	76.7	74.2
25–29 years	76.1	73.4
30–34 years	74.9	72.0
35–39 years	73.1	70.7
40–44 years	68.9	68.2

Although similar declines occurred among white females, the proportion of white husbands present never dropped below 90 per cent except for the first and last age group.

Nearly One-Quarter of Negro Births Are Now Illegitimate

Both white and Negro illegitimacy rates have been increasing, although from dramatically different bases. The white rate was 2 per cent in 1940; it was 3.07 per cent in 1963. In that period, the Negro rate went from 16.8 per cent to 23.6 per cent.

The number of illegitimate children per 1,000 live births increased by 11 among whites in the period 1940–63, but by 68 among nonwhites. There are, of course, limits to the dependability of these statistics. There are almost certainly a considerable number of Negro children who, although technically illegitimate, are in fact the offspring of stable unions. On the other hand, it may be assumed that many births that are in fact illegitimate are recorded otherwise. Probably the two opposite effects cancel each other out.

On the urban frontier, the nonwhite illegitimacy rates are usually higher than the national average, and the increase of late has been drastic.

In the District of Columbia, the illegitimacy rate for nonwhites grew from 21.8 per cent in 1950, to 29.5 per cent in 1964.

A similar picture of disintegrating Negro marriages emerges from the divorce statistics. Divorces have increased of late for both whites and nonwhites, but at a much greater rate for the latter. In 1940 both groups had a divorce rate of 2.2 per cent. By 1964 the white rate had risen to 3.6 per cent, but the nonwhite rate had reached 5.1 per cent —40 per cent greater than the formerly equal white rate.

Almost One-Fourth of Negro Families Are Headed by Females

As a direct result of this high rate of divorce, separation, and desertion, a very large per cent of Negro families are headed by females. While the percentage of such families among whites has been dropping since 1940, it has been rising among Negroes.

The per cent of nonwhite families headed by a female is more than double the per cent for whites. Fatherless nonwhite families increased by a sixth between 1950 and 1960, but held constant for white families.

It has been estimated that only a minority of Negro children reach the age of 18 having lived all their lives with both their parents.

Once again, this measure of family disorganization is found to be diminishing among white families and increasing among Negro families.

The Breakdown of the Negro Family Has Led to a Startling Increase in Welfare Dependency

The majority of Negro children receive public assistance under the AFDC program at one point or another in their childhood.

At present, 14 per cent of Negro children are receiving AFDC assistance, as against 2 per cent of white children. Eight per cent of white children receive such assistance at some time, as against 56 per cent of nonwhites, according to an extrapolation based on HEW data. (Let it be noted, however, that out of a total of 1.8 million nonwhite illegitimate children in the nation in 1961, 1.3 million were *not* receiving aid under the AFDC program, although a substantial number have, or will, receive aid at some time in their lives.)

Again, the situation may be said to be worsening. The AFDC program, deriving from the long established Mothers' Aid programs, was established in 1935 principally to care for widows and orphans, although the legislation covered all children in homes deprived of parental support because one or both of their parents are absent or incapacitated.

In the beginning, the number of AFDC families in which the father was absent because of desertion was less than a third of the total. Today it is two-thirds. HEW estimates "that between two-thirds and three-fourths of the 50 per cent increase from 1948 to 1955 in the number of absent-father families receiving AFDC may be explained by an increase in broken homes in the population."

✿   ✿   ✿

The steady expansion of this welfare program, as of public assistance programs in general, can be taken as a measure of the steady disinte-

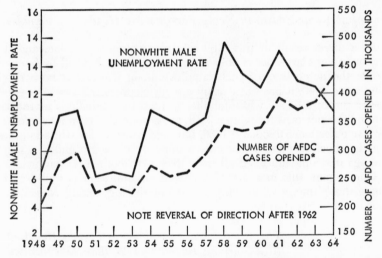

* Does not include cases opened under program which commenced in some states in 1961 of assistance to children whose fathers are present but unemployed.

Cases opened under AFDC compared with unemployment rate for nonwhite males

gration of the Negro family structure over the past generation in the United States.

✿   ✿   ✿

THE CASE FOR NATIONAL ACTION

The object of this study has been to define a problem, rather than propose solutions to it. We have kept within these confines for three reasons.

First, there are many persons, within and without the Government, who do not feel the problem exists, at least in any serious degree. These persons feel that, with the legal obstacles to assimilation out of the way, matters will take care of themselves in the normal course of events. This is a fundamental issue, and requires a decision within the Government.

Second, it is our view that the problem is so inter-related, one thing with another, that any list of program proposals would necessarily be incomplete, and would distract attention from the main point of inter-relatedness. We have shown a clear relation between male employment, for example, and the number of welfare dependent children. Employment in turn reflects educational achievement, which depends in large part on family stability, which reflects employment. Where we should break into this cycle, and how, are the most difficult domestic questions facing the United States. We must first reach agreement on what the problem is, then we will know what questions must be answered.

Third, it is necessary to acknowledge the view, held by a number of responsible persons, that this problem may in fact be out of control. This is a view with which we emphatically and totally disagree, but the view must be acknowledged. The persistent rise in Negro educational achievement is probably the main trend that belies this thesis. On the other hand our study has produced some clear indications that the situation may indeed have begun to feed on itself. It may be noted, for example, that for most of the post-war period male Negro unemployment and the number of new AFDC cases rose and fell together as if connected by a chain from 1948 to 1962. The correlation between the two series of data was an astonishing .91. (This would mean that 83 per cent of the rise and fall in AFDC cases can be statistically ascribed to the rise and fall in the unemployment rate.) In 1960, however, for the first time, unemployment declined, but the number of new AFDC cases rose. In 1963 this happened a second time. In 1964 a third. The possible implications of these and other data are serious enough that they, too, should be understood before program proposals are made.

However, the argument of this paper does lead to one central conclusion: Whatever the specific elements of a national effort designed to resolve this problem, those elements must be coordinated in terms of one general strategy.

What then is that problem? We feel the answer is clear enough. Three centuries of injustice have brought about deep-seated structural distortions in the life of the Negro American. At this point, the present tangle of pathology is capable of perpetuating itself without assistance from the white world. The cycle can be broken only if these distortions are set right.

In a word, a national effort towards the problems of Negro Americans must be directed towards the question of family structure. The object should be to strengthen the Negro family so as to enable it to raise and support its members as do other families. After that, how this group of Americans chooses to run its affairs, take advantage of its opportunities, or fail to do so, is none of the nation's business.

DECLINE IN THE RELATIVE INCOME
OF NEGRO MEN

Alan B. Batchelder

Migration from the South to other regions of the country has been a major source of improvement in the incomes of American Negroes. Professor Batchelder demonstrates that except for high rates of Negro migration from the South, the earnings of Negro males would have declined relative to the earnings of white males during the decade 1950–1960. Even so for the nation as a whole Negro males were only able to hold their own relative to white males during the decade. Alan B. Batchelder is a Professor of Economics at Kenyon College and is currently on sabbatical leave in Liberia with the Harvard Development Advisory Service.

It is a commonplace that racial barriers have put the American Negro in a position that has allowed him, on the average, to produce and to lay claim to a smaller per capita share of America's real output than the white American. This article examines statistical data showing the economic position of American Negroes relative to whites in 1949 and in 1959. The particular statistics used are the median annual income figures for Negroes and for whites. Two questions are raised and answered, at least in part; these are: First, given the racial turbulence of the 1950's, did the American Negro's relative income position decline, hold steady, or improve during the fifties? Second, what explanations can be found for the changes that took place, particularly the changes for men?

Ratios aside, the real per capita income of American Negroes has been rising on the wings of rising American productivity. However,

From "Decline in the Relative Income of Negro Men," by Alan B. Batchelder, *The Quarterly Journal of Economics*, 78, No. 4 (November, 1964), 525–48. Excerpted and reprinted by permission of *The Quarterly Journal of Economics* and Alan B. Batchelder.

assuming that income comparisons with a man's peers are more mean-
ingful than income comparisons with his progenitors, the focus of
attention in this article will be on secular changes in the Negro-white
income ratio, rather than on secular changes in Negro income alone.

✳   ✳   ✳

In 1950 the Census Bureau began the decennial collection of per-
sonal income data. Only now, with income statistics available by
race and region from the 1950 and 1960 censuses, is it possible to
use income data to measure secular changes in the economic position
of Negroes relative to whites.

✳   ✳   ✳

INCOME DATA FOR MEN, 1949 AND 1959

In Table 1 the median income of Negro men is compared with
the median income of white men for the years 1949 and 1959. Dollar
figures appear for each group, and the ratio of Negro to white
income is also shown as a percentage. Separate figures are presented
for the conterminous United States (a Census Bureau expression re-
ferring to the 48 States other than Hawaii and Alaska) and for each
of the four major census regions. The income concept used here
comprises three parts: wage and salary income, self-employment in-
come, and "other" income, the latter including rent, interest, dividends,
and transfer receipts. . . .

Between 1949 and 1959, the median dollar income of each group
in each area rose. However, attention here centers upon what hap-
pened to the ratio of male Negro to male white income; that is to
say, what happened to the economic position in America of the
Negro as compared with the white primary breadwinner. For the
country as a whole, the Negro's position showed no change, standing
at 52.52 per cent of the white's in 1949 and 51.96 in 1959. In both
years Negro men were able to bring home, on the average, in earn-
ings and other income only slightly more than one half of what white
men were able to bring home. In income terms, the relative economic
position of American Negro men was low in 1949 and no higher in
1959.

These are national data. When viewing them, one must bear in
mind that, between 1950 and 1960, 1,457,000 nonwhites (most of
whom were Negroes) moved out of the South and into the North
and West. One must also remember, as Table 1 shows, that the 1949
data for regions (and the 1959 data as well) show the ratio of male
Negro to male white income to have been much lower in the South
than in the other three regions. Therefore, given the size of the
Negro movement out of the South, where Negro income was and is

TABLE 1

*Median Income of Negro Men and Median Income of White Men,
1949 and 1959: Dollar Amounts and Ratios, for the Conterminous
United States and by Region*

Region	Dollar Income[1] Negro over White		Income Ratio, Negro to White	
	1949[2]	1959[3]	1949	1959
Conterminous United States[4]	$1,334 / $2,572	$2,254 / $4,337	52.52	51.96
Northeast	2,061 / 2,759	3,326 / 4,623	74.70	71.94
North Central	2,210 / 2,721	3,468 / 4,525	81.22	76.64
West	2,049 / 2,786	3,395 / 4,773	73.55	71.13
South	1,033 / 2,065	1,643 / 3,524	50.02	46.62

[1] For males 14 years old and over reporting 1949 or 1959 income. . . . *U.S. Census of Population: 1950*, II: *Characteristics of the Population*, Part 1, *U.S. Summary*, p. 63. *U.S. Census of Population: 1960, Detailed Characteristics, U.S. Summary*, p. XXXIX.

[2] Conterminous United States: *U.S. Census of Population: 1950*, II: *Characteristics of the Population*, p. 1–297; regions: white income—same volume, pp. 1–413–414; Negro income computed by the author from data for individual states—same volume, Table 87 of Parts for the several states. Based on a 20 per cent sample.

[3] *U.S. Census of Population: 1960, Detailed Characteristics, U.S. Summary*, pp. 1–578, and 1–734–736. Based on a 25 per cent sample.

[4] The forty-eight states other than Hawaii and Alaska.

quite small compared with white, and into the North and West, where the income ratio is nearer unity, one would expect, *ceteris paribus,* a substantial rise in the Negro-to-white ratio for the nation as a whole simply as a consequence of the shift in weighting. That this rise did *not* follow was the consequence of a *decline* in the relative income position of Negro men within every one of the four major census regions.

The values of these declines were 2.42 points in the West, 2.76 in the Northeast, 3.40 in the South, and 4.58 in the North Central States. Thus it may be said of any particular region that in income terms the relative position of Negro men was low in 1949 and still lower in 1959.

Furthermore, these statistics do not result from averaging together figures for many states, in some of which the Negro position declined, in some of which the Negro position improved. Herman P. Miller, Special Assistant to the Director of the Bureau of the Census, appeared before a Congressional committee in July 1963. He said that in the 26 states (including the District of Columbia) which have 100,000 or more Negroes, the ratio of Negro to white income for males increased between 1949 and 1959 in only two states (District of Columbia and Florida).* In two others (New Jersey and Oklahoma), it was unchanged. In every other state there was a widening of the gap between the incomes of whites and Negroes, and in some cases the increase was fairly substantial. Given this consistent decline throughout America in the relative income position of Negro men, it may seem surprising that the income experience of Negro women during the 1950's was quite different.

INCOME DATA FOR WOMEN, 1949 AND 1959

During the 1950's, there was a narrowing of the gap between the income of Negro women and the income of white women. Table 2 presents the dollar figures for median income of white women and Negro women in 1949 and in 1959 for the conterminous United States and for each census region. Table 2 also presents the Negro-white income ratios for women in each region in 1949 and in 1959. For the nation, the Negro position advanced from 51 to 60 per cent of the white. In the three non-Southern regions, Negro women's income drew within three or four percentage points of white women's income. Even in the South, the percentage gap between Negro and white women was reduced.

*   *   *

WHY THE RELATIVE DECLINE FOR NEGRO MEN?

As mentioned earlier, the income data comprise three parts: wage and salary income, self-employment income, and "other income," the latter including dividends, interest, rent, and transfer payments. It is upon the first two parts that the present inquiry will now concentrate. This concentration does not imply any lack of interest by the author in the income flows included in the third income component. Rather it is that the national and regional data deriving from the Census Bureau are limited to variables chiefly affecting wages, salaries, and (this to a lesser extent) self-employment income. Prop-

* H. P. Miller, *Statement before the Subcommittee on Employment and Manpower, U.S. Senate Committee on Labor and Public Welfare,* U.S. Bureau of the Census, mimeo (Washington, D.C., 1963), p. 6.

TABLE 2

Median Income of Negro Women and Median Income of White Women, 1949 and 1959: Dollar Amounts and Ratios, for the Conterminous United States and by Region

Region	Dollar Income,[1] Negro over White		Income Ratio, Negro to White	
	1949[2]	1959[2]	1949	1959
Conterminous United States	$ 581 / $1,137	$ 905 / $1,509	51.10	59.97
Northeast	1,165 / 1,407	1,724 / 1,748	82.80	98.63
North Central	938 / 1,086	1,355 / 1,393	86.37	97.27
West	920 / 1,008	1,543 / 1,612	91.27	95.72
South	440 / 947	732 / 1,317	46.46	55.58

[1] For females 14 years old and over reporting 1949 or 1959 income.
[2] Source: Same as Table 1.

erty income and transfer payments may have been important as causes of the relative decline in male Negro income, but they will not be examined here. . . .

Considering variables operating chiefly through wages and salaries, the 1949–59 regional declines in the income position of Negro men relative to that of white men could have been due to a decline in the quality of the male Negro as compared with the male white labor force; it could have been due to an increase in the quantity of the male Negro as compared with that of the male white labor force; or it could have been due to increased discrimination against Negroes by white employers. An explanation may also be sought in more immediate causes; as compared with white men, Negro men may have experienced greater growth in unemployment, greater growth in the importance of part-time workers, greater growth in the importance of casual and intermittent workers, or shifts from more to less well-paid jobs.

In the sections below, median age of men in the labor force and median years of school completed by men aged 16 and over will be used to measure relative trends in the quality of the male Negro and the male white labor forces. To measure relative quantity, the size of the Negro labor force will be compared with the size of the entire labor force. Finally, consideration will be given to unemployment rates, part-time workers, and occupational distribution as immediate causes of the decline in the relative income status of Negro men.

The results of this examination will indicate for each region particular variables associated with the 1949–59 decline in the relative income position of Negro men. In the South growing unemployment among Negro men relative to white men and increased concentration of Negro men in laboring and service occupations will appear as the chief reasons for the decline.

In the North and West the explanatory variables derive from the Negroes out-migration from the South. This movement increased the supply of Negroes relative to the supply of whites in the Northern and Western male labor force and, quite possibly, depressed the educational level of Northern and Western Negro men relative to Northern and Western white men. It is curious, however, to find that similar causes for Negro women did not result in similar income effects as between Negro and white women. In the North and West no evidence of declining economic status for Negro men is to be found in the occupational data. Together, therefore, the occupational and income data suggest that in the North and West job changes unfavorable to Negro men occurred within rather than among the occupational categories used by the Census Bureau.

*   *   *

TRENDS IN THE SIXTIES

What has happened since 1959? On the basis of a sample, the Census Bureau, once each year, estimates median annual money income for men and for women, for whites and for nonwhites. These data are published in the *Current Population Reports* Series, P-60. If use is made of three year averages centering upon 1949 and upon 1959, the figures from this source yield nonwhite-to-white income ratios of .52 for 1949 and .50 for 1959 for men and of .45 for 1949 and .61 for 1959 for women. These figures are remarkably similar to those shown in Tables 1 and 2. The two sources for income data agree in showing a decline, during the fifties, in the Negro-to-white (or nonwhite-to-white) income ratio for men and an increase for women.

And in more recent years? The nonwhite-to-white income ratio for men averaged .50 for 1958–60 and fell to .49 for 1962. The ratio for women averaged .61 for 1958–60 and rose to .67 for 1962. The trends of the 1950's continued.

*   *   *

CONCLUSION

Becker and Rayack* used occupational indices to show that during the 1940's, a decade distinguished by its tight labor market, the Negro's occupational position moved nearer that of whites. During the 1950's, the press reported the fall of many racial barriers. Yet income data show that during this decade of relatively weak demand (and despite the migration of 1,457,000 Negroes out of the South and into the relatively high income North and West) there was no increase between 1949 and 1959 in the national Negro-to-white median income ratio for men. This is because within each of the four census regions, there was a decline in the Negro-to-white median income ratio for men.

It remains to be seen what the decade of the sixties will permit. The current population report samples indicate that the trends of the fifties continued at least through 1962. Whatever happens, economists will continue to be interested in the Negro-to-white median income ratio because, given the assumption that the average male white and the average male Negro are born with equal ability, an "efficient" allocation first of resources to education and second of men to work would result in an equal average contribution to production by (and equal income for) Negro men and white men. The data presented in this paper indicate that the equal-contribution ideal grew more rather than less chimerical during the decade of the fifties.

The social significance of that decade lay in the circumstance that while the press spoke of progress the gap grew between the income of Negro and white men, and the Negro man's economic dependence upon Negro women increased. Surely this talk of progress added to the frustration of men who experienced no progress.

Great moral fervor was directed against discrimination in the 1950's, but the labor market was much weaker in the fifties than in the forties. Therefore the question: Can exhortation ever be as effective a means to Negro advance as is buoyant demand? The trends of the sixties seem to remain those of the fifties. In the years ahead, buoyant demand may return, civil rights legislation may exert unprecedented leverage, or exhortation may gain in effectiveness; but if none of these possibilities materializes, the trends of the sixties may remain the trends of the fifties. If so there will be an economic justification for the "fire next time."

* G. S. Becker, *The Economics of Discrimination* (Chicago: University of Chicago Press, 1957), and Elton Rayack, "Discrimination and the Occupational Progress of Negroes," *Review of Economics and Statistics*, XLIII (May 1961), 209–14.

INVESTMENT IN THE HUMAN RESOURCES OF NEGROES

Barbara R. Bergmann

Investments in human capital are a critical determinant of life-time earnings. Part of the large gap in Negro and white earnings is attributable to the smaller quantity of human capital invested in the average Negro than in the average white. Barbara R. Bergmann, an Associate Professor of Economics at the University of Maryland, estimates that the value of the stock of human capital embodied in the average male adult Negro is on the order of $10,000 smaller than the human capital embodied in the average white male. These estimates include both the value of human capital acquired through schooling and on-the-job training.

It is well known that Negroes, as a group, are possessed of less of the education, training, and experience needed to enter into and perform well in high-paying, high-productivity occupations than are whites. In years past, dollars which should have been invested in enhancing Negroes' ability to be economically productive—in building up "human capital" of Negroes—were not invested, in part because of discrimination, and in part because of the poverty and ignorance of many of the Negroes themselves. The result is that the value of the stock of human capital embodied in the average male adult Negro is on the order of $10,000 smaller than the human capital the average white male has possession of. For the nation as a whole, this adds up to a deficiency of around $50 billion of investment in the human capital of adult male Negro Americans, which would have been made had they been whites.

From "Investment in the Human Resources of Negroes," by Barbara R. Bergmann, in U.S. Congress, Joint Economic Committee, *Federal Programs for the Development of Human Resources,* Vol. 1, Part II, *Manpower and Education* (Washington, D.C.: Government Printing Office, 1968). Reprinted by permission of the author.

The estimating procedure which produced these numbers is admittedly a rough one, but even if the errors are on the order of 100 per cent, the conclusion must be the same: the cost to the nation of repairing past errors of omission and commission toward Negroes is very large. The Negro deficiency of "human capital" is not the sole reason that many Negroes have low incomes and live in dilapidated housing, but it undoubtedly is a major reason for their lower standard of living. Even if discrimination against Negroes, as Negroes, were to cease entirely and immediately, the largely justified discrimination against the uneducated and inexperienced on the part of those who decide who are to occupy the higher paying jobs would deprive Negroes of an equal share in the good things of American life.

The heart of Negro disabilities is the fact that Negroes are underrepresented in the higher paying, higher productivity jobs. Some of this underrepresentation could be remedied immediately, given the willingness of whites to do so. There are many jobs for which only whites are hired currently which could be filled by Negroes, since the supply of Negro labor fit to fill them already exists, unemployed or doing lower paid work. For example, a considerable number of Negro foremen could undoubtedly be found among Negro production workers who have been passed over previously for only racial reasons. Those willing to hire Negroes for sales jobs seem to have found no difficulty in finding well-spoken, well-appearing Negroes, as a visit to many large department stores in many northern cities will confirm. Some supermarkets, when pressed, were able to come up with Negro checkers. Many banks were able to find Negroes suitable for teller's jobs. There is no reason to believe that other stores, supermarkets, and banks could not, if they wished, do the same, or that the number of Negro teamsters could not be expanded rapidly without lowering the qualifications.

On the other hand, there are job categories where adequate representation of Negroes could not be achieved now, or even 10 years from now. These are jobs in which considerable formal training is required and/or in which a worker must be "aged" by on-the-job experience. Obvious extreme examples are physicians and upper level company executives. These are jobs in which the required investment in "human resources" is very large. While comparatively few occupational classes require as much human investment as do physicians, such investments do play a large part in the structure of American job holding. Thus the fact that Negroes have embodied in them less "human capital" than do other groups will require rectification if they are to be integrated into all levels of the economy.

When we consider the kind of programs needed to repair the large deficiency in investment in human capital of Negroes, it is clear that we must both prevent underinvestment in the new generation of Negro children, and we must repair, to the extent possible, the damage to older Negroes. These older Negroes, whose capital deficiencies form the basis of the estimates quoted above, will be harder to help, in the sense that the amount of investment in them necessary to raise their incomes significantly may be prohibitively large. For older Negroes, then, rectification of their condition may in considerable part have to consist in Government-supplied income supplements rather than in "dividends" earned on an enhanced stock of human capital.

The formation of human capital takes place in schools, at the workplace where valuable experience is gained, in the physician's office or hospital where health deficiencies which lower productivity are dealt with, and even in the home, where attitudes and habits which affect work performance are ingrained. In our estimate of Negroes' deficiency in human capital, we shall deal only with the first two sources of investment where the imponderables are fewest, and where the bulk of the capital is formed.

. . . The mean number of school years completed by whites [in 1960] was 10 years, while for nonwhites the mean was 7.3 years. The difference of 2.7 years represents a major part of the deficiency of human investment. Moreover, as of 1960, 79 per cent of Negroes had been born in the Southeast, an area notorious for low educational spending. In 1963 the Southern States on the average spent $305 per pupil per year, as compared with an average of $473 for the rest of the country. As we go further back in history, the comparison between expenditures per pupil in the South and in the rest of the country grows worse. For example, in 1929–30, all of the Southeastern States with the exception of West Virginia failed to spend as much as half of the national average of $87 per pupil. Furthermore, the existence of segregated schools in the South means that the deficiency was compounded. In 1952, expenditures per pupil for white and Negro schools in the South were $165 and $115 respectively, while in 1940, when many of the present adults were children, the comparable figures were $50 and $22.

The assembly of these figures into a single estimate of the deficiency of educational investment in Negroes is complicated by difficulties in interpreting the rise in costs which have occurred and by the lack of information as to where Negroes actually received their education. Furthermore, some of the Negro educational gap is represented by lack of college training, in which the costs are more than twice those of lower schools. We shall thus rest content at valuing the 2.7 missed years of school for Negroes at $400 per year, which is roughly their replacement cost now and counting the deficiencies in quality at $60 per year. This seems like a minimal estimate, even when the desirability of introducing a depreciation factor is included. When we apply this to the 4.7 million male Negroes who were 25 or over in

1960, we arrive at a total capital deficiency in the neighborhood of $7 billion.

A second major source of human capital formation in which Negroes have built up deficient shares is in the area of work experience. If we consider census data on mean income of males in 1960 by age, education, and race, and take the figures for a given educational level, it is possible to trace out the effect on income of age, which presumably represents the effect of experience. For example, white college graduates reach their peak earnings in the 45 to 54 age bracket, at which time they are earning $6,400 more than men of similar education in the 25 to 34 age bracket. Negro college graduates start with lower pay and get smaller increases in income with experience. The advance between the 25 to 34 and 45 to 54 age brackets is only about $1,000 for them.

Both the lower starting salary and the lower increases due to experience for Negroes reflect discrimination and the fact that Negro and white education are not on a par. However, a major cause of the failure of Negro workers to advance in salary with age to the extent that whites do is that the nature of the jobs to which they are restricted is such as to limit the value of experience. A man who sweeps the floor may be no more productive at 45 than at 25, or may be less productive; a man with the same education who starts as an operative may gain skill and may go on to supervisory work as he ages.

TABLE 1

Mean Income of Males 25 to 64 Years Old in the Experienced Labor Force by Race, Age, and Years of School Completed, 1960

Race and age	Years of school completed					
	Elementary		High school		College	
	0 to 7	8	1 to 3	4	1 to 3	4 or more
White:						
25 to 34	$3,537	$4,357	$4,998	$5,480	$5,964	$ 7,146
35 to 44	4,015	4,861	5,671	6,507	8,007	11,027
45 to 54	4,093	5,000	5,852	6,793	8,752	13,536
55 to 64	4,088	4,908	5,874	6,940	8,760	13,300
Nonwhite:						
25 to 34	2,151	2,844	3,136	3,657	4,078	4,439
35 to 44	2,444	3,362	3,740	4,266	4,623	5,479
45 to 54	2,436	3,396	3,591	4,017	4,312	5,482
55 to 64	2,284	3,211	3,394	3,780	3,998	5,108

Source: *1960 Census of Population: Occupation by Earnings and Education.*

TABLE 2

*Estimated Capital Value of Experience of Males 25 to 64 Years Old
in the Experienced Labor Force by Race, Age, and Years of School
Completed, 1960*

[*In Thousands of Dollars*]

Race and age	Years of school completed					
	Elementary		High school		College	
	0 to 7	8	1 to 3	4	1 to 3	4 or more
White:						
25 to 34	$2.5	$2.7	$ 3.6	$ 5.5	$10.9	$20.6
35 to 44	7.2	7.6	10.2	15.5	30.9	58.6
45 to 54	6.9	8.2	10.2	15.7	32.7	70.7
55 to 64	3.8	3.7	5.8	9.5	18.3	38.5
Nonwhite						
25 to 34	1.6	2.8	3.2	3.2	2.8	5.5
35 to 44	4.1	7.6	7.9	7.4	5.2	15.0
45 to 54	3.0	6.1	5.7	4.6	1.0	11.7
55 to 64	1.2	2.8	2.6	1.8	.6	5.3

Source: Computed on the basis of data in *1960 Census of Population: Occupation
by Earnings and Education.*

It is possible to use the census data on incomes to capitalize the
value of experience for each group homogeneous by education, age,
and race. As with income, the capital values also reach a peak and
then fall, representing the fact that earnings tail off toward the end
of worklife, but also and more importantly representing the fact that
a man in the highest age bracket (55–64) has on the average only
5 more years to receive dividends on the experience-capital he has
built up.

When we take a weighted average of the capital values of experience
estimated, we arrive at a figure for whites of $13,912 and for Negroes
of $4,049, a difference of $9,863. It is interesting to note that weight-
ing Negroes experience-capital values by the distribution of whites
as to age and education raises the average of Negro capital value to
only $4,978, demonstrating that the observed difference in average
capital values is in large part independent of educational differences.
This further leads to the conclusion that this aspect of underinvest-
ment of Negroes can be corrected, for younger groups at least, by a
radical conversion of the country to desegregation of employment.

The total capital deficiency due to denial of experience to Negroes
is about $42 billion, on this calculation.

In summary, we may remark that the rough calculation of the value of the human capital deficiency of Negroes as compared with whites which is presented here is to some degree also a rough and partial measure of what Negroes are "owed" by American society. To the extent possible, it should be "paid" by a rapid buildup in the human capital of Negroes, so that they may be enabled to earn on a more comparable basis with whites.

THE ECONOMIC COST
OF DISCRIMINATION

Council of Economic Advisers

*In 1965 the Council of Economic Advisers presented estimates of
the economic cost of discrimination in their annual report. They
reported that Negroes had not been participating fully in the abun-
dance of the nation's economy. "On the average, they have less edu-
cation, work in less skilled occupations, suffer more unemployment,
and get paid lower wages." This CEA staff memorandum explains
the derivation of these estimates.*

A White House press release dated March 25, 1965, contained
estimates of the economic cost of discrimination from a report to the
President by the Council of Economic Advisers. This memorandum
explains the derivation of those estimates.

1. *If Negroes received the same average pay as whites having the same
   education, the personal income of Negroes and of the Nation would be
   $12.8 billion higher.*
   Using 1960 Census data, the number of employed Negroes was calcu-
   lated by level of education, area of residence (urban, rural nonfarm,
   and rural farm), and sex. These figures were multiplied by the incomes
   of white workers in the same categories. By comparing these adjusted
   incomes with the actual incomes of Negroes in 1960, it was possible
   to compute the percentage increase in total personal income that
   would have resulted from the elimination of discrimination in employ-
   ment. When applied to 1964 personal income levels, the result was
   $12.8 billion.
2. *If Negroes also had the same educational attainments as white workers,
   and earned the same pay and experienced the same unemployment as*

"The Economic Cost of Discrimination" (editor's title). From a staff memo-
randum of the Council of Economic Advisers (March 26, 1965, mimeographed).

whites, their personal income—and that of the Nation—would be $20.6 billion higher.

Using 1960 Census data, the male and female Negro population was standardized to the white population by assuming that Negroes had the same level of education, the same employment rates, and the same geographic distribution as whites. These standardized Negro employment and population figures were multiplied by the incomes of white persons in the same categories. The percentage income gain was computed by comparing these adjusted incomes with that of the actual income of the Negro population in 1960. At 1964 personal income levels this would yield an increase of $20.6 billion.

3. *The entire economy would benefit from better education of Negro workers and an end to job discrimination. Industry would earn additional profits. The total Gross National Product would rise by an estimated $23 billion, or an extra 3.7%.*

The extra $7.8 billion ($20.6–$12.8) gain in personal income that results from assuming the Negro population to have the same education, employment rate, and location, involves an assumed investment in human resources, and a resulting rise in productivity of Negro workers. As a result, the increase in Gross National Product (GNP) would be larger than the increase in personal income. Multiplying the $7.8 billion by the ratio of total personal income to total GNP, yields an extra $2.2 billion in GNP. Therefore, the over-all increase in GNP in the absence of racial discrimination would be about $23 billion ($20.6 + $2.2).

ON THE COST OF BEING A NEGRO

Paul M. Siegel

Paul M. Siegel, Professor of Sociology at the University of Michigan, provides estimates of what discrimination means to the individual Negro. Using data from the 1960 Census of Population, he examines white-nonwhite differentials in average earnings within major occupation groups at every educational level. He estimates that being a Negro costs about $1000 on the average. Few birthrights come so high.

Prior to the publication of the 1960 Census of Population, simultaneous tabulations of income by education *and* occupation were not available apart from small sample surveys. Tabulations of this kind are now available, specific to region and race, for a five per cent sample of the male civilian experienced labor force aged 25–64 in 1960. These data provide a unique opportunity for examining white-nonwhite differentials in average earnings within major occupation groups at every educational level, for both the South and the non-South (which will be called the North). Figures 1 to 4 show the relationship between mean earnings in 1959 and educational attainment separately for whites and nonwhites in the North and South. A separate figure is presented for each Census major occupation group; a capital N is used to identify curves for nonwhites and a capital W identifies those for whites; and solid lines indicate incomes in the North while dashed lines indicate those in the South.

The pattern of relationships illustrated in Figures 1 to 4 is remarkably consistent. [The original paper contains illustrations for all 10 industry categories.] With the single exception of nonwhite farmers in the North, the figures show that at *every* educational level in every occupational group, and in the North as well as the South, nonwhites

From "On the Cost of Being a Negro," by Paul M. Siegel, *Sociological Inquiry*, 35, No. 1 (Winter, 1965), 41–58. Excerpted and reprinted by permission of *Sociological Inquiry* and Paul M. Siegel.

*Mean Income of 25–64 Year Old U.S. Males of the Experienced Labor Force in Each Occupational Category at Different Levels of Education, by Race and Region.**

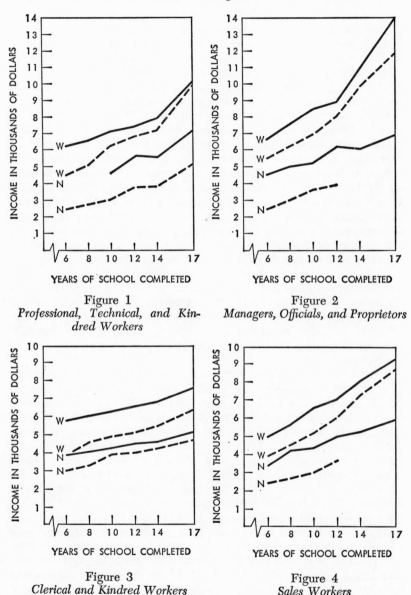

Figure 1
Professional, Technical, and Kindred Workers

Figure 2
Managers, Officials, and Proprietors

Figure 3
Clerical and Kindred Workers

Figure 4
Sales Workers

* Note for Figures 1–4: Occupational categories are those used by the U.S. Census. Dotted lines represent the Southern United States; solid lines describe the balance of the country. "W" and "N" refer to white and nonwhite, respectively.

have average earnings less than those of whites. This finding has long been anticipated but until the appearance of the 1960 Census data it was not possible to demonstrate it comprehensively. The figures also enable one to see the magnitude of the differentials, which are frequently in excess of a thousand dollars. Indeed, not only are differences of this magnitude observed between white and nonwhite earnings within each of the geographic regions under consideration: differences in excess of $1000 are observed between the earnings of nonwhites in the South and nonwhites elsewhere in the United States.

While one might choose to interpret these differences as due to quality differences in education, or to differences in detailed occupational distributions within major occupation groups, it seems unlikely that either factor alone, or both in conjunction, could produce differentials as large as those shown in the charts. This point is perhaps amply documented by reading some of the more dramatic differentials from the charts. For example, Figure 1 shows that a white professional in the North, with fewer than eight years of school completed, earns on the average a thousand dollars more per year than a nonwhite professional in the South with four or more years of college. Figure 2 indicates that on the average a nonwhite Northern manager who has completed four or more years of college earns no more than his white counterpart with less than eight years of school completed. This latter difference reflects, no doubt, the etiquette of retail relationships, wherein Negro managers are largely restricted to servicing Negro clientele and are restricted from achieving supervisory positions superior to whites. Other striking contrasts can be found in each of the figures.

Many of the striking contrasts one can extract from the figures might of course be "explained away" by differences in the detailed occupational pursuits of whites and nonwhites within major occupational categories. But since we have previously argued that at some educational levels Negroes cannot *get* the same jobs as whites, to invoke detailed occupational differentiation of those Negroes who do gain employment comparable with that of their white educational peers is to change the argument from "Negroes are paid less than whites with the same training in the same jobs," to "Negroes are not allowed into the high paying jobs within major occupational groups." The latter argument could be buttressed by reference to the rules of race relations which exclude Negroes from positions of authority over whites, or from entry into trades governed by discriminatory unions. The point is, of course, that the income differentials displayed in Figures 1 to 4 do not necessarily reflect white-nonwhite pay differentials for similar work and similar training: various features of the social organization of the relations between the races may also account for the differentials. But regardless of what final account is given of the differentials here displayed, an individual Negro cannot expect to earn as much as a white person with the same number of years of school completed and at the same general level of employment.

Inspection of the figures also reveals that the white-nonwhite differentials in earnings at most occupational and educational levels are greater inside than outside the South. Although the differential is occasionally as great as $1000, for most occupation-education combinations the white-nonwhite income difference is on the order of $100 to $500 greater in the South.

Apart from racial and regional differences in income, we can also derive some understanding of how the occupational structure itself affects the differential incomes of Negroes and whites. All of the figures are plotted in the same scale, so comparisons between them can readily be made. Comparisons of this kind will show that the differentials between whites and nonwhites average least among clerical and kindred workers, service workers, and unskilled laborers. Since these are the very levels at which one might expect the detailed occupations of whites and nonwhites to be most similar, these comparisons tend to confirm our previous suspicion that part of the white-nonwhite income differential observed at the higher status occupational levels reflected differences in detailed occupational affiliation.

Close inspection of the figures also reveals that there is both a general tendency for income to increase with education and two sub-tendencies: (1) for income to increase *more* rapidly with increasing education in some occupations than in others; and (2) for white-nonwhite *differentials* to increase with increasing education. The general tendency and the first sub-tendency indicate that there is what can be thought of as a return on investment in education and that the return on this investment is higher in professional, managerial, sales, and craft occupations than among the other major occupational categories, excluding farmers and farm managers (a special case). This is not too surprising: the payoff on investment in education is conditioned by the relevance of the training to the kind of work performed. One can easily see that in this respect the white and nonwhite occupational hierarchies are roughly parallel. This phenomenon is, of course, quite relevant to the matter at hand, for it is from the very occupations at which the return upon investment in education is greatest that Negroes find themselves excluded by rules governing the *social context* of the practice of occupations. Thus we conclude that the Negro who manages to upgrade himself educationally is apt to find the occupational door closed at the levels of employment which enable him to realize his investment in educational attainment, a conclusion to which we have been drawn before.

The tendency for income differentials between whites and nonwhites to increase with increasing education holds both inside and outside the South. . . . Statistically the pattern means that the slope of the regression of income on education within occupational categories will be less for nonwhites than for whites. Substantively the divergence implies that the return in income for completing a given educational step is less for nonwhites than it is for whites. Since they are independent, if we compare the slopes of the curves for whites and nonwhites at each educational step, within regions and major occupational groups, we can summarize the patterns of return upon investment in education by counting the number of comparisons in which the income increment for completing a given educational step is larger for whites than for nonwhites. Within the South there are 33 such comparisons. In 29, or 87.2 per cent of these 33 comparisons the increment in average earnings for completing a given education step is less for nonwhites than for whites. The pattern for the North is equally striking: in 34, or 82.9 per cent of the 41 comparisons in the North, the increment in average earnings for completing a given educational step was larger for whites than for nonwhites. These findings suggest, barring serious errors of reporting which could account for the observed pattern, that the rate of return upon educational investment is appreciably less for Negroes than for whites. Thus the Negro not only starts out with a financial handicap, but in most occupations the handicap is *accentuated* with increasing education.

In order to summarily display this disadvantageous aspect of increasing education, we present in the first column of Table 1 the mean white-nonwhite earnings difference for each of six levels of educational attainment for all occupations and regions. While the tabled values clearly show that the difference between white and nonwhite earnings increases with increasing education, differences in occupational and regional distributions—shown in the figures to account for sizeable white-nonwhite earnings differences—are not taken into account in the first column of the table. A simple procedure will enable us to remedy this confounding.

We begin by noting that for all males aged 25–64 in the experienced civilian labor force with earnings in 1959 and with, for example, less than eight years of education, the difference between the average earnings of whites and nonwhites was $1421. This is a gross figure and in no way takes account of occupational or residential differences between the two groups. We can, by simple algebraic manipulation of the differences of these two mean incomes, decompose it into two terms: one term expressing that part of the total difference attributable to white-nonwhite differences in regional and occupational composition (tabulated as the "mean difference attributable to composition"), and the other term expressing that part of the total difference attributable to white-nonwhite earnings differences specific to occupa-

TABLE 1

Decompositions of Mean Differences Between White and Nonwhite
Earnings in 1959 for Males Aged 25–64 in the United States, 1960,
Specific to Education Groups*

Years of School Completed	Mean Difference White-Nonwhite Earnings	Mean Difference Attributable to Occupa-tional-Regional Composition	Mean Difference Net of Composition	Mean Nonwhite Earnings
Elementary 0–7 years	$1,421	$ 725	$ 696	$2,562
Elementary 8 years	1,519	601	918	3,318
High School 1–3 years	2,033	757	1,276	3,522
High School 4 years	2,229	823	1,406	4,021
College 1–3 years	3,199	1,441	1,758	4,355
College 4 or more years	4,567	767	3,800	5,671

* Source: U.S. Bureau of the Census, *U.S. Census of Population: 1960, Subject Reports, Occupation by Earnings and Education,* Washington, D.C.: U.S. Government Printing Office, 1963. Table 1.

tion region (the "mean difference net of composition").* This particular formula is not unique; it is only one of numerous similar relationships which enable one to ascertain the components of a difference between two rates.

Working out the suggested decomposition of the total earnings difference among those with less than eight years of schooling, we see

* Letting W represent mean income to whites and w represent mean income of nonwhites, we can represent the gross mean difference by:

$$(1) \quad W - w = \sum_{i,j} N_{ij}W_{ij} - \sum_{i,j} n_{ij}w_{ij}$$

Where N_{ij} is the proportion of all whites who are in the ith region (South or non-South) and the jth occupation, and n_{ij} and w_{ij} are the corresponding proportions and mean wage rates for nonwhites and the summation is over all combinations. The value $W - w$ will not be changed by adding and then subtracting the same term, so we can write

$$(2) \quad W - w = \sum_{i,j} N_{ij}W_{ij} + \sum_{i,j} n_{ij}W_{ij} - \sum_{i,j} n_{ij}W_{ij} - \sum_{i,j} n_{ij}w_{ij}$$

This can be regrouped and rewritten thus:

$$(3) \quad W - w = \sum_{i,j} n_{ij}(W_{ij} - w_{ij}) + \sum_{i,j} W_{ij}(N_{ij} - n_{ij})$$

Note that the first term on the right-hand side of (3) is merely the sum over all nonwhites of white-nonwhite mean earning differences within region and occupation. The second term on the right side of (3) is the portion of the gross differences due to compositional differences. See Evelyn M. Kitagawa, "Components of a Difference between Two Rates," *Journal of the American Statistical Association*, 50 (December, 1955), pp. 1168–1194.

that $725 of the total difference of $1421 can be attributed to differences in the proportions of whites and nonwhites in particular occupational-regional categories. On the other hand $696 of the total difference in white-nonwhite earnings can be attributed to white-nonwhite differences in rates of earnings within region and occupation combinations for this particular educational group. These rate differences can be interpreted as reflecting the money costs to nonwhites of discrimination, though they may to some extent be influenced by quality differences in education or occupation which are too fine to be discerned by our gross measures. It is quite apparent in Table 1 that, while earnings differences due to composition do not vary systematically with education, when the effects of occupational and regional composition are removed the remaining earnings differences increase regularly as level of educational achievement increases. This means that, even if whites had the same occupational and regional configuration as nonwhites, there would remain rather large income differences; and these would be accentuated with increasing education.

*   *   *

The data provide no support for the view that education will immediately remove the financial and occupational handicaps imposed on the Negro. On the contrary, they suggest that increasing the level of educational attainment of the Negro may lead to higher white-nonwhite income differentials, at least in the short run. Since this is a statement about longitudinal trends inferred from cross-sectional data, it is intended to be taken with great caution. However, the data certainly warrant the conclusion that there is no closing of the income gap at higher levels of education.

Findings like these clearly suggest part of what current racial protest movements are about. Before we proceed to assess the import of these objective relations in terms of the subjective processes that underlie race relations, it might be well to attempt to provide a single figure which expresses the impost referred to in the title of this paper.

We have thus far avoided the question of the cost of being a Negro for two reasons. First, we wanted to demonstrate that white-nonwhite income differentials appear at most educational and occupational levels and that little progress in occupational desegregation has been made since 1940. These findings, of course, imply that the cost of being a Negro is itself a variable. Consequently, any single figure must be an average taken over widely different circumstances. Second, we avoided preparing such an estimate because *any* evaluation of the average cost of being a Negro is necessarily arbitrary at certain points owing to (1) decisions about methods of calculation and (2) limitations imposed by the available data. Although the estimate we present below has some appeal, it ignores differences in white-nonwhite age structure and of course, suffers from being taken over major instead of detailed occupational categories. Therefore, it must be treated as but one of several such estimates that could be made.

We have already discussed the method by which we shall estimate the cost of being a Negro, for it consists of modifying the decomposition equation already discussed to take account of education as a compositional variable in addition to occupation and region. Applying this new equation to the mean difference in white-nonwhite earnings for the total population of males aged 25–64 with earnings in 1959, we shall again derive two terms, one corresponding to the amount of the difference attributable to occupational, educational, and regional differences between the two groups, and the other expressing the difference in earnings net of composition. We shall interpret this second term as the cost of being a Negro.

Working out the suggested decomposition of the total difference in average white-nonwhite earnings, we find that only $1097 of the total difference of $2852 can be attributed to white-nonwhite differences in mean earnings within region, occupation, and education combinations. Thus, net of regional, educational, and occupational effects, the cost of being a Negro is roughly a thousand dollars. On the other hand, 61.5 per cent of the total difference in white and nonwhite mean earnings can be attributed to compositional differences with regard to region, occupation, and education. This suggests that the current discrepancy might be appreciably reduced if Negroes could bring their educational, occupational, and geographical distribution more into line with that of whites. We have tried to argue here that changes along the first two dimensions would *not* be particularly efficacious, and there are good arguments that equalization of the geographic distributions of the races would not ameliorate the income distributions. In any case such herculean metamorphoses would not eliminate income differentials—for 38.5 per cent of the current difference in average earnings of whites and nonwhites is apparently *independent of the achievement* of nonwhites! To put it baldly, about two-fifths of the difference in average earnings of whites and nonwhites is what it costs to be black.

*   *   *

As the majority of Negroes interviewed by a *Newsweek* poll put it, "if you do the same work as a white man, you will probably be paid less than he will." And, we can now say how much less: about a thousand dollars a year.

PART II

The Labor Market

THE CHANGING POSITION
OF NEGRO WORKERS

Dale L. Hiestand

The concentration of Negroes in low status and low paying occupations has been an important part of the pattern of discrimination and low incomes experienced by Negroes since emancipation. Professor Hiestand traces the changes in the occupational patterns of Negro and white workers between 1910 and 1960 in an effort to determine whether there is more or less equality between their occupational distributions now than in the past. Dale L. Hiestand is an Associate Professor of Business at the Graduate School of Business, Columbia University, and a Senior Research Associate of the Conservation of Human Resources Project at Columbia.

. . . How do changes in the occupational patterns of minority groups —and, again, specifically of Negroes—compare with the patterns of the white labor force? Is there more or less equality between the occupational distributions of Negro and white workers now than in the past? . . . We will attempt to answer these questions for the half century, 1910 to 1960.

THE CHANGING OCCUPATIONAL DISTRIBUTION
OF NEGRO AND WHITE WORKERS

In 1910, . . . half of the Negro labor force was engaged in farming, as compared to only 28 per cent of the white labor force. As the

From "The Changing Position of Negro Workers," in *Economic Growth and Employment Opportunities for Minorities,* by Dale L. Hiestand (New York: Columbia University Press, 1964), pp. 41–57. Copyright © 1964 by Columbia University Press. Excerpted and reprinted by permission of Columbia University Press and Dale L. Hiestand.

economy grew and labor resources were increasingly transferred to the nonfarming sector, Negroes made the transition even more rapidly than white workers. As a result, in 1960 a great discrepancy no longer prevailed; farming then claimed 7 per cent of the white labor force and 11 per cent of the Negro labor force. This great transfer is nearing its end, however, for rural areas can no longer continue to supply major amounts of manpower to other sectors.

A new discrepancy prevailed in 1960, but in the manual and service occupations. The proportion of the white labor force in this sector of work has been remarkably stable since 1910; it has remained at just under 50 per cent. As the proportion of white workers in farming declined, their proportion in the white collar sector increased by almost exactly the same amount. In effect, there was a transfer from farming to white collar work of over 20 per cent of the white labor force.

In contrast, as Negroes turned away from farming, they found opportunities primarily in the manual and service occupations. In 1910 less than half of all Negroes were in manual and service work, as were almost half of all white workers. In the succeeding decades the proportion of Negroes in this sector climbed steadily to nearly three fourths in 1960, a much larger proportion than among white workers.

White collar work was not an important field for Negro employment for many decades, but recently this has changed. Only 3 per cent of Negro workers were engaged in white collar occupations in 1910, 6 per cent in 1940, and 15 per cent in 1960. We see, then, that the shift in the Negro labor force prior to 1940 was almost wholly from farming to manual and service work. Since then the transfer has been divided; white collar jobs have been as important as manual and service work as growing areas of Negro employment.

Over the long run, of course, the major transformation for Negroes has been the increased importance of manual and service work. In 1910 unskilled labor and service occupations were the principal nonfarm fields for Negroes and accounted for 38 per cent of the total. These fields increased in importance between 1910 and 1930, when they included almost half of all employed Negroes, and they have remained at this level. Within these fields unskilled labor has remained at a relatively stable level since 1940, accounting for about one out of seven Negro workers.

Since 1940 the operative occupations have been primarily responsible for the continued growth of the proportion of Negroes in blue collar work. Only 5 per cent of Negro manpower was employed as semiskilled workers in 1910. This proportion increased to 10 per cent in 1940, nearly doubled in the next decade to 18 per cent, and increased to 21 per cent by 1960. The operative occupations have become the major field of work for Negroes.

The 1940s also marked a slight increase in the relative importance of skilled work as a field of employment for Negroes. Between 1910 and 1940 the proportion of Negroes in such work increased by less than 1 per cent. This proportion increased from 3 to 5.5 per cent between 1940 and 1950 and has increased slightly since.

As noted earlier, most of the increase in the importance of the white collar occupations for Negro employment has also occurred since 1940. This increase occurred primarily in the clerical and sales occupations, to a lesser extent in the professional and related occupations, and hardly at all in proprietary and managerial employment. Less than 1 per cent of all Negro workers were in clerical and sales work in 1910 and only 2 per cent in 1940. This proportion increased to 5 per cent by 1950 and 8 per cent in 1960. The increase in the importance of the professions and subprofessions as fields of Negro employment has been slow, from 1 per cent of the total in 1910 to 3 per cent in 1940 and 1950 and nearly 5 per cent in 1960. The change in the employment of Negroes as proprietors and managers has been insignificant.

*   *   *

AN INDEX OF RELATIVE OCCUPATIONAL POSITION

There is no clear-cut answer to the question of whether Negro men and women now have a greater degree of occupational equality relative to white men and women than they had in the past. The data suggest strongly that this is so, however. In every field but one, there are now more Negroes, both men and women, relative to the number of whites than there were formerly. The exception is farming, but Negroes have always been overrepresented in this sector. An overall answer involves a conclusion as to whether the trend toward equality in the various white collar and skilled fields is more or less important than the trend toward greater inequality in unskilled labor and, to a lesser extent, in service work; it involves also an assessment of the fact that in the semiskilled field Negro men have moved from a position of underrepresentation to overrepresentation.

One way to do this has been suggested by Gary S. Becker, who devised an index of relative occupational position in which the different occupational groups are considered more or less important according to the average income level in them. By applying constant income weights to the changing occupational distribution of each population group, a set of indexes of absolute occupational position can be developed for various dates. By comparing these, conclusions can be reached as to whether Negroes have advanced occupationally more or less rapidly than whites.

The present analysis is somewhat more extensive than Becker's. He divided the occupational structure into three groups: skilled, including all white collar workers and craftsmen and foremen; semiskilled; and unskilled, including nonfarm laborers, service workers, and farm laborers. He excluded farmers and farm tenants from his calculations on the ground that it is difficult to classify or compare the skills of whites and Negroes in this occupation. The index becomes more sensitive to occupational shifts, the greater the number of groups that are used. Therefore, our indexes are based on seven occupational groupings: professional and related workers; nonfarm proprietors, managers, and officials; clerical and sales workers; skilled workers, or craftsmen and foremen; semiskilled workers, or operatives; service workers and nonfarm laborers; and farmers and farm workers.

Combining farmers and farm laborers avoids the question that Becker raised of the uncertain skill classification of farmers. We do not know, of course, how skilled the Negro farm work force is relative to the white farm work force, but this defect of the index applies to every occupational group. Among those employed as semiskilled workers or operatives, for instance, white workers have been heavily concentrated in manufacturing, while Negroes have been primarily employed as truck drivers, laundry and dry cleaning workers, and the like. In the professional category white men have been heavily concentrated in engineering, law, medicine and related professions, and these contain very few Negroes. Education and the clergy, the chief fields for Negro professionals, also contain many white men, but the relative skill levels of whites and Negroes in these fields, particularly in the past, may also be questioned. We also want to include farmers because for both whites and Negroes the transfer from agriculture was truly an occupational advancement.

The present set of indexes compares white and Negro men, as did Becker. The analysis is also extended, by comparisons of white versus Negro women, male versus female whites, and male versus female Negroes. The indexes are computed for every ten years over the past half century, and they fill in earlier dates that Becker omitted and extend the series to 1960. The income weights are from the 1950 Census and are a weighted average of the median incomes for men and women in the various occupational groups who worked at least fifty weeks during the previous year; Becker used 1939 weights.

Despite the elaborate recalculation of the data, the essential conclusions reached by Becker are reconfirmed here. They are also extended in several directions. Table 1 presents the results.

The occupational position of Negro men relative to that of white men changed little between 1910 and 1940. Significant gains were made in the 1940s when an improvement of 5 per cent was achieved. Whether 1910 or 1940 is used as a base, the position of Negro men

TABLE 1

*Index of Occupational Position of Negroes Relative to White Workers,
by Sex, and of Females Relative to Males, by Race, 1910–1960*

	1910	1920	1930	1940	1950	1960
Occupational position of Negroes relative to whites:						
Male	78.0	78.1	78.2	77.5	81.4	82.1
Female	78.0	71.3	74.8	76.8	81.6	84.3
Occupational position of females relative to males:						
White	101.4	110.0	105.6	102.6	98.9	93.6
Negro	101.5	99.9	101.0	101.7	99.3	96.1

relative to that of white men had improved by approximately 6 per
cent by 1960, wiping out approximately one fifth of the gross differ-
ential that had existed between them.

FINDINGS RE WOMEN

The occupational position of Negro women relative to white women
has taken a somewhat different course. Their relative position suffered
during the 1910–20 decade as great numbers of white women entered
clerical and sales work. Since 1920, however, the position of Negro
women has advanced steadily by about 4 to 6 per cent per decade.
Despite the decline in the first decade, the position of Negro women
relative to white women improved by 8 per cent during the half
century, wiping out more than one fourth of the differential. Between
1920 and 1960 the relative position of Negro women improved by
18 per cent, wiping out nearly half of the differential.

We have noted that the question of "occupational equality" is not
the same as "economic equality." The latter concept involves trends
not only in occupational changes but also in wage structures. Because
of the long-range tendency for wages in the semiskilled, unskilled, and
service categories to increase at a more rapid rate than those in the
skilled, professional, and managerial fields and because Negroes are
concentrated at the bottom of the occupational ladder, they have un-
doubtedly obtained far greater relative advances in income than have
whites. In addition, many of the returns from work now come as
fringe benefits, but changes in their relative importance for Negroes
and whites are as yet unknown. Finally, much more income now comes
in the form of social security and other governmental payments and
in such public services as education, recreation, housing, transporta-
tion, medical services, etc. To assess the degree to which Negroes have

moved toward equality in all these aspects extends far beyond an occupational analysis.

Purely from the point of view of occupational equality, the advances of Negroes relative to whites cannot be considered remarkable, even if we consider only the period since 1940. The remaining discrepancies between the Negro and white occupational positions—and these indexes understate them by ignoring intraclass differences—are so great that the prospects of substantial equality during the present century are not particularly promising. During the 1950s practically all of the net growth in nonfarm employment among white men occurred at the skilled level or above; nearly half the growth occurred in professional and technical occupations, more than one fourth in other white collar jobs, and nearly all of the remaining fourth in the skilled category. Among Negro men, on the other hand, only two fifths of the net growth in employment in the 1950s occurred in the skilled or white collar occupations; over one third was in unskilled labor. These discrepancies, largely reflecting the differing education, skills, and opportunities of the young, will influence the measures of over-all occupational equality between the races for nearly half a century to come. And, despite the current civil rights efforts, there are little prospects that all the differences between whites and Negroes in terms of their regional and residential patterns, their backgrounds, and in the way employers, unions, and others in the labor market treat them will soon be erased. There are, therefore, little prospects that we will soon see substantial equality in the education, skills, and opportunities of the new groups of young people of the two races.

EMPLOYING NEGROES IN URBAN
LABOR MARKETS

Walter H. Powell

Many employers seeking to hire qualified Negroes have discovered that their traditional methods of recruiting and selection are inadequate. Walter Powell, Vice President of the International Resistance Corporation, discusses some of the special problems of recruiting Negro workers, even when there is a strong commitment by management to do so. In making these observations he draws heavily on the experiences of his company.

IMPERFECTIONS IN THE LABOR MARKET

In terms of employer efforts to recruit Negroes at any level of the skill ladder, employers generally know nothing about the Negro community and the Negro labor market. On the other side of the coin, the Negro community (whatever nebulous group that might be) neither knows about the availability of jobs nor how to advise its unemployed on the methods of a job search. There is presently no contact point nor effective channel through which to reach Negro applicants. When an employer continually states that a Negro has never applied to his company, it is not a prima facie case of discrimination. There are many companies which would welcome Negro applicants, but they do not know how to attract Negro candidates for employment. This is especially true of the smaller employer.

Even though the environment to encourage Negro employment has been growing ever since World War II, companies trying to comply with the fair employment acts of city, state, and federal government

From "Employing Negroes in Urban Labor Markets," by Walter H. Powell. Excerpted and reprinted from *The Negro and Employment Opportunity: Problems and Practices,* ed. Herbert R. Northrup and Richard L. Rowan (Ann Arbor, Michigan: Bureau of Industrial Relations, 1965) by permission of the Bureau of Industrial Relations, The University of Michigan.

cannot yet find adequate numbers of eligible Negroes for their job openings. Companies with collective bargaining agreements that are obligated by contract to post all vacancies and promotional opportunities on bulletin boards are bewildered in that their own Negro employees do not take advantage of the opportunities for promotion or upgrading. Further, Negro employees, as a rule, do not recommend their friends or relatives for the job vacancies that are posted within their own companies.

In the case of our own company, we have a practice of posting nearly all salaried as well as the hourly jobs. The rationale is obvious. The referral of friends by our employees makes an excellent potential labor supply. In spite of this practice, for the past ten years and with a high Negro population within the company, the number of referrals has been so negligible as to be not even worth discussing.

As a company, we have continually advertised in the local newspapers with "open" advertisements, and even the inclusion of the statement that we are an "Equal Opportunity Employer" has not significantly increased gate applications. And this is in a community where we, as a company, have been identified with fair employment practices, where we are active members of the Urban League, and have maintained strong relationships with many interracial groups. How then does one penetrate the urban labor market? The urban labor market is imperfect. The communications are poor. Prejudices and fears are hampering the meeting of the forces of supply and demand. It is a job market in which the Negro has made very substantial numerical gains in employment but poor progress in merit employment. There are other factors that must be studied to determine whether or not the changes in the pattern of employment have been sufficient to warrant an optimistic attitude toward the Negroes' industrial future. In the 1940's, the outlook was none too rosy because discrimination was quite prevalent. During the 1950's, even though there was an erosion of prejudice, it would be naive to say it had disappeared. However, in the 1950's and 1960's, with the pressures of federal and state legislation, opportunities for Negro advancement in industry began to open up.

Merit employment was the driving theme of progressive and militant Negro organizations. This was a deviation from merely hiring Negroes for traditional jobs. As the 1940's matured into the 1950's and 1960's, stability and length of employment provided the Negro with sufficient seniority to withstand the variations in the business cycles. However, there has not been a tremendous amount of upgrading in industry among this group with comparatively low seniority. A comparison of this group with a similar grouping of white semi-skilled workers, employed about the same time, will not show that one group has advanced at the expense of the other.

The opportunities were for unskilled and semi-skilled jobs and not for skilled and managerial positions, and the persons filling those jobs did not have the attributes to be promoted.

In the latter part of the forties and through the fifties until today, the well-educated Negro trained in business skills has primarily sought employment in civil service. The protective nature of government employment against prejudice, and against the unknown, has provided a haven for competent Negroes. Thus, a heavy segment of the Negro population which is capable of being upgraded in industry is not within the ranks of industry. There are several explanations of this phenomenon. First, the jobs available during the war years were mainly unskilled and semi-skilled jobs. Second, the normal channels for securing white collar jobs have been closed to the Negro until recently. Third, the Negro has hesitated—and been reluctant—to take on responsibility in lower managerial jobs such as factory supervision. The reasons are sociological, economic, and psychological, and, while disturbing, they are not surprising. The Negro employee has not availed himself of the opportunities of apprentice training and upgrading guaranteed to him under most collective bargaining agreements.

Unfortunately, the heavy trend to civil service and government work for white collar jobs has meant under-employment for many capable people. Upgrading is possible, but the competition is probably more intense within the limited environmental factors of government than within the whole of industry. Efforts to dislodge this group from these cloistered jobs into the mainstream of industry have failed continually. . . .

Within the past two months, our company went into the labor market twice to find male, semi-skilled employees. More specifically, the job specifications called for men who could read, write, and perform with training, jobs of janitor, warehouseman, material handler, and molder. Twenty work days are more than enough to train the average candidate for any of these positions.

The advertisements were placed in the two Philadelphia Sunday papers. We stated the name of the company, its address, and the fact that it is an "Equal Opportunity Employer." We stated that once an employee completes his initial qualification period, he is eligible to bid for any open job posted on the bulletin board. Thus, within the framework of the union-management agreement, we attempt to encourage free movement upward for all individuals. (Parenthetically, it is not surprising that we restrict lateral moves and downgrades and encourage promotions.)

As an initial condition for hiring employees, we think in terms of upgrading. It is not enough to hire a man as a sweeper in the lowest wage grade, because sooner or later he will want advancement, and it is to our advantage for him to be promoted. As part of our pre-employment procedure, we have established certain hiring agreements that are basic to all jobs.

The response to our advertising was exceptionally good. Over one hundred men appeared, but only seventy-six were processed. The others left without completing the application for employment. Almost 85 per cent of the applicants were colored. Out of the seventy-six men, we were only able to hire four immediately, and six are possible future call-ins.

Our recruiting and screening practice included giving a verbal or non-verbal intelligence test, seeking a minimum standard comparable to an eighth-grade education. We also gave four simple arithmetic questions calling for simple addition and subtraction skills. Two right was considered qualifying. A fourth- or fifth-grade student should be able to do all four correctly.

Eighteen of the seventy-five failed the test. Fifteen failed to complete all parts of the test. Twenty-seven could not get past the interviewer, either because of poor work history or attitude.

This pattern is not unusual; it has been repeated several times within our limited sphere of activity. Other companies in the Philadelphia community have had similar experiences that have taxed their facilities and their good intentions.

RACIAL INEQUALITY IN EMPLOYMENT: THE PATTERNS OF DISCRIMINATION

Herbert Hill

Discriminatory practices by employers and unions bear a major share of the responsibility for the continued existence of the pattern of racial job discrimination. State and federally financed manpower programs also have a direct responsibility for the perpetuation of the low occupational status and earnings of Negro workers. Herbert Hill, National Labor Director for the NAACP, describes these discriminatory practices, with particular emphasis on those prevalent in Southern labor markets.

Optimistic assumptions regarding the Negro's progress in American society must be re-examined in the light of the Negro's current economic plight. The great mass of Negroes, especially in the urban centers, are locked in a permanent condition of poverty. This includes the long-term unemployed as well as the working poor, who know only a marginal economic existence and who increasingly are forced into the ranks of the unemployed.

❋　　❋　　❋

THE NEGRO IN THE SOUTH

All the evidence indicates that in the Southern states there exists a rigid and systematic pattern of employment discrimination based on race. Industrial management and organized labor, as well as state agencies and the federal government, are responsible for the continued existence of the pattern of racial job discrimination. An immense in-

From "Racial Inequality in Employment: The Patterns of Discrimination," by Herbert Hill, *The Annals of the American Academy of Political and Social Science,* 357 (January 1965), 30–47. Excerpted and reprinted by permission of The American Academy of Political and Social Science and Herbert Hill.

dustrial development has been taking place in the southeastern states since the end of World War II, but a most disturbing aspect of the rapid growth of manufacturing facilities in the South has been the serious inability of the Negro worker to register significant employment gains in the new Southern industrial economy.

Investigations indicate that in the textile industry, still the basic manufacturing industry of the South, Negroes are in a most marginal position. According to state government figures, the number of textile workers employed in South Carolina was 48,000 in 1918 and 122,000 in 1960, while the percentage of Negroes in the textile labor force fell from 9 per cent to 4.7 per cent over this period. On July 6, 1961, the National Association for the Advancement of Colored People filed an extensive series of complaints against major textile manufacturing companies with the President's Committee on Equal Employment Opportunity. Three years later there is little change in the racial occupational pattern in the Southern textile industry. Negroes remain concentrated in menial and unskilled classifications and comprise about 2 per cent of the work force.

＊   ＊   ＊

On April 6, 1962, in an appraisal of the first year of operation of the President's Committee on Equal Employment Opportunity the NAACP stated:

The administration has relied for favorable publicity on a superficial approach called "Plans for Progress." The so-called "Plans for Progress"—voluntary agreements entered into by a few large corporations—may yield high returns in press notices but only superficial and token results for Negro workers in new job opportunities. The "Plans for Progress" have not produced the large scale job opportunities for Negro workers that have been so long denied them. It is our experience that major U.S. Government contractors operating vast multi-plant enterprises regard the signing of a "Plan for Progress" as a way of securing immunity from real compliance with the antidiscrimination provision of their government contract.

＊   ＊   ＊

In heavy industry, the gains of Negro labor throughout the Southern states are most limited. Negro employment is negligible in such major industrial operations as the General Motors plants in Atlanta and Doraville, Georgia, and the Ford Motor Company plants in Atlanta, Memphis, Norfolk, and Dallas. The employment study made by the United States Commission on Civil Rights confirms our opinion that very little progress has been made by the Southern Negro in heavy industry. The Commission's findings are summarized in part in its published report as follows:

This Commission's investigations in three cities—Atlanta, Baltimore and Detroit—and a Commission hearing in Detroit revealed that in most industries studied, patterns of Negro employment by Federal contractors conformed to local industrial employment patterns. In Atlanta, the two automobile assembly plants contacted employed no Negroes in assembly operations. Except for one driver of an inside power truck, all Negro employees observed were in janitorial work—sweeping, mopping, carrying away trash. Lack of qualified applicants cannot account for the absence of Negroes from automotive assembly jobs in Atlanta. Wage rates are relatively high for the locality and the jobs are in great demand. The work is at most semi-skilled and educational requirements are extremely low.[1]

A major problem for Negro workers in Southern industry is the operation of separate racial seniority lines in collective bargaining agreements entered into by management and labor unions. Investigations of the status of Negro workers in pulp and papermaking operations, in chemical and oil refining, in steel and tobacco manufacturing, as well as in other important sectors of the Southern industrial economy, clearly indicate that Negroes are usually hired exclusively in classifications designated as "common laborer" or "yard labor" or "nonoperating department" or "maintenance department." These are the euphemisms for the segregated all-Negro labor departments established by the separate racial promotional lines in many labor-management contracts throughout Southern industry. As a result of these discriminatory provisions, white persons are initially hired into production or skilled craft occupations which are completely closed to Negro workers. The Negro worker who is hired as a laborer in the "maintenance department" or "yard labor department" is denied seniority and promotional rights into desirable production classifications and is also denied admission into apprentice and other training programs. In these situations Negro seniority rights are operative only within certain all-Negro departments, and Negro workers therefore have an extremely limited job mobility. Thus Donald Dewey, of Columbia University, reports that most Southerners believe that their economy is divided into "white" and "Negro" jobs.[2] The North Carolina Advisory Committee to the United States Commission on Civil Rights reports that, "North Carolina in common with states of its region, has traditions which more or less automatically assign Negroes to menial or unskilled positions." [3]

The pulp and papermaking industry is one of the fastest growing manufacturing industries in the South. Company management and the trade unions which have jurisdiction in this important Southern industry are responsible for a rigid pattern of discriminatory practices including separate racial promotional lines in union contracts which limit Negro workers to menial, unskilled job classifications at low pay and which violate their basic seniority rights. The two dominant unions in this industry are the United Papermakers' and Paperworkers' Union and the International Brotherhood of Pulp, Sulphite and Paper Mill Workers' Union, both affiliated with the AFL-CIO. In virtually every paper mill in the South where they hold collective bargaining agreements, these two unions operate segregated locals and include discriminatory provisions in their union contracts. A compelling example of the operation of segregated locals with separate racial seniority lines is to be found at the large manufacturing plant of the Union Bag-Camp Paper Corporation in Savannah, where thousands of persons are employed. This plant has the largest single industrial payroll in Savannah.

The tobacco industry is important in the Southern industrial economy, and here, too, we find a pattern of separate racial seniority lines in virtually all collective bargaining agreements between the major tobacco manufacturing companies and the Tobacco Workers International Union, AFL-CIO. In one of the largest manufacturing plants, that of the Liggett & Myers Tobacco Company in Durham, North Carolina, colored workers are employed in unskilled and janitorial jobs with limited seniority rights operative only in all-Negro designated classifications. Investigations made by the NAACP indicate that in this tobacco manufacturing plant, as in so many others, Negroes are initially hired only as sweepers, janitors, and toilet attendants and are promoted exclusively within the limited "Negro" seniority line of progression.

Negro railway workers throughout the South are the victims of a traditional policy of job discrimination as a result of collusion between railway management and railroad labor unions. In St. Petersburg, the Atlantic Coast Line Railroad, and, in Memphis, the St. Louis-San Francisco Railroad Company, for example, have entered into agreements with the Brotherhood of Railroad Trainmen to deny qualified Negro railway workers opportunities for promotion and advancement. These are typical of similar practices elsewhere.

The Brotherhood of Railroad Trainmen, an AFL-CIO affiliate, removed the "Caucasian Only" clause from its constitution in 1959. However, this was apparently for public relations purposes only, as the union continues in most cities to exclude qualified Negro railroad employees. Frequently, in collusion with management, Negro brakemen are classified as "porters" and then refused membership in the union under the pretext of their being outside its jurisdiction. This, however, does not prevent the Trainmen's Union from negotiating wages and other conditions of employment for these so-called "porters" who have no representation in the collective bargaining unit.

STATE EMPLOYMENT SERVICES

Another extremely serious problem confronting Negro workers is the discriminatory practices of state employment services whose operation, in Southern states, is characterized by a pattern of racial segregation and discrimination. These states include Alabama, Florida, Georgia, Louisiana, Mississippi, North Carolina, South Carolina, and, partially, Virginia and Tennessee. Job orders are racially designated, and job referrals are made on the basis of race. Major industrial corporations operating with federal government contracts cannot possibly be in compliance with the President's Executive Order banning employment discrimination where such contractors in the South are using the facilities of the state employment services. The United States government is completely responsible for providing the operating costs of all state employment services. Federal funds are disbursed by the Department of Labor, which administers the Federal-State Employment Services program. It obviously makes no sense for the Administration to issue executive orders banning employment discrimination by government contractors while agencies of the federal government subsidize such discriminatory practices. . . .

FEDERAL SUPPORT OF DISCRIMINATION

Even in the North, the operation of the state employment services represents a serious problem to Negro workers. . . . A further problem is the usual tacit assumption by local employment service personnel that there are "white" jobs and "colored" jobs. This is a result of the prevailing hiring pattern in many localities and the reluctance of state employment services to innovate changes in the established racial patterns.

Because the colored worker is extremely vulnerable to long-term unemployment as a result of the combined factors of racial discrimination and technological change, Negro workers more than any other group in the work force qualify for training under the Federal Manpower Development and Training Act. However, investigations made by the NAACP clearly indicate that Negroes, with some few exceptions, are being limited to programs that simply perpetuate the traditional concentration of Negroes in menial and unskilled jobs. Thus, in Portland, Oregon, there was an all-Negro training program for hotel waiters, and in Pensacola, Florida, there were all-Negro programs for chambermaids and waitresses. In Birmingham, Alabama, there are all-white training programs in electronics and arc welding, but Negroes are limited to training as laundry-machine operators and shirt-pressers. In Beaufort, South Carolina, there is a training program for Negro waiters, while in Greenville, South Carolina, there is an all-white program for general machine and tool machine workers. The *Courier-Journal*, Louisville, Kentucky, December 11, 1962, in a news report headlined "200 Retrainees Can't Get Jobs" states: "One course was held for Negro clerk-stenographers but it developed that employers in that area wanted only white clerical help."

* * *

The Department of Health, Education, and Welfare each year distributes fifty-five millions of dollars of federal funds for education under the Smith-Hughes Act; a very large part of this is given to vocational training programs in which Negroes are totally excluded or limited to unequal segregated facilities. Vocational and trade schools in the Southern states receive a substantial part of these federal funds, but in most Southern urban areas where there has been a tremendous growth of manufacturing operations, we find that the limited programs offered in Negro vocational schools are obsolete in terms of modern industrial technology. Thus, while white students in vocational schools are preparing for advanced technology in electronics and for the automotive and aero-space industries, Negroes are limited to "home economics" and other traditional service occupations, and here also the federal government has a direct responsibility for helping to perpetuate the pattern that makes the Negro worker an unskilled worker and most vulnerable to large-scale permanent unemployment.

* * *

APPRENTICESHIP AND VOCATIONAL TRAINING

For many occupations the only way a worker can be recognized as qualified for employment is to successfully complete apprenticeship training programs. This is true for the printing trades, among machinists and metal workers, in the various crafts in the building and construction trades industry, and many others.

Studies such as that made by the New York State Commission Against Discrimination,[4] as well as by the National Association for the Advancement of Colored People, clearly indicate that no significant advances have been made by Negroes in those craft union apprenticeship training programs which have historically excluded nonwhites. An examination of the available data makes it evident that less than one per cent of the apprentices in the building and construction industry throughout the United States are Negro. In the ten-year period, 1950–1960, in the State of New York, the increase of Negro participation in building trades apprenticeship programs rose from 1.5 per cent to 2 per cent.

Open access to plumbing and pipe fitting apprenticeship controlled by the Plumbers Union is a very rare experience for young Negroes in the North as well as the South. Similarly, Negro youths are excluded from apprenticeship programs controlled by the Sheet Metal Workers Union, the International Brotherhood of Electrical Workers, the Lathers and Plasterers Union, the Boilermakers, the Structural Iron Workers Union, and from other important craft unions operating in the construction industry.

Almost equally exclusive are the printing trades unions. In a survey made by the National Association for the Advancement of Colored People of the seven major New York City newspapers in 1962, we find that, with the exclusion of building services and maintenance personnel, less than one per cent of those employed on the major New York newspapers are Negro. Virtually all of the Negroes employed on these newspapers are in the "white collar" jurisdiction of the New York Newspaper Guild.

It is estimated that in New York City less than one half of one per cent of those currently employed in the newspaper crafts outside the Guild's jurisdiction are Negroes. This includes printing pressmen, compositors, photoengravers, stereotypers, paper-handlers, mailers, and delivery drivers. As far as apprenticeship training for these crafts are concerned, we have been unable to detect a single instance where Negroes have been recently admitted into a training program in the newspaper crafts in the City of New York or in other major cities in the United States.

*   *   *

Labor unions also exercise control over apprenticeship programs through hiring hall procedures in de facto closed shop situations. In these circumstances, craft unions have the power either to promote or to prevent the admission of individuals or of an entire class of persons. By means of a variety of formal and informal controls, craft unions are frequently the decisive factor in the recruitment process in many apprenticeship programs and often directly prevent Negro youth from becoming skilled craft workers via the established route of apprenticeship.

On the level of the small shop and local union, the tradition of racial discrimination has now become deeply institutionalized. A form of caste psychology impels many workers to regard their own positions as "white man's jobs," to which no Negro should aspire. These workers, and often their union leaders, regard jobs in their industries as a kind of private privilege, to be accorded and denied by them as they see fit. Often Negroes are not alone in being barred from such unions which have much of the character of the medieval guild, but Negroes as a group suffer the most from these practices. On the local level, the tradition which sustains discrimination is to be found among skilled workers in heavy industry as well as in the craft occupations, and in the North almost as commonly as in the South.

The Bureau of Apprenticeship and Training of the United States Department of Labor, in giving certification to an apprenticeship program, provides the legal basis for public subsidies to apprenticeship programs. The federal government, through grants-in-aid from the United States Office of Education of the Department of Health, Education, and Welfare, provides funds which subsidize apprenticeship training programs in many states. The federal government, therefore, is directly subsidizing discrimination in the skilled trades whenever a trade union or employer excludes Negroes and members of other minority groups from admission into a registered apprenticeship training program.

*   *   *

THE RACIAL PRACTICES OF ORGANIZED LABOR

Even some unions which boast of a "liberal" past are under attack for discriminatory racial practices now that large numbers of Negroes have entered their jurisdiction. On April 4, 1961, a complaint was filed by Ernest Holmes, a Negro worker, against the International Ladies' Garment Workers Union (ILGWU) with the New York State Commission for Human Rights, the agency that administers the state's fair employment practices statutes. The ILGWU was accused of discriminatory practices involving Negro workers. Later investigations revealed that nonwhites in the New York garment industry were concentrated in the lowest-paid job classifications with very little job mobility, because, with some few exceptions, they were denied admission into the union's skilled craft locals, that the virtually all-Negro and Puerto Rican "push boys" unit known as 60A is in practice a "jim crow" auxiliary, and that not a single Negro was an International Union officer, or on the 23-man executive board, or permitted to serve in any significant leadership position.[5]

*   *   *

It is of some significance to note that this was not the first encounter by the ILGWU with the New York State antidiscrimination agency. Eighteen years ago the ILGWU entered into an agreement with the New York State Commission Against Discrimination—the predecessor to the State Commission for Human Rights—that it would not bar Negroes, Spanish-speaking, or other persons from membership in the all-Italian locals (*Elsie Hunter* v. *Agnes Sullivan Dress Shop*, September 4, 1946). . . .

. . . Today, eighteen years later, not a single Negro or Spanish-speaking person holds membership in the two Italian locals which have control of some of the highest paying jobs in the industry, and no action has been taken to comply with the state law forbidding such practices.

Currently, the Negro worker is confronted not with a trade union movement that is a force for social change, but, on the contrary, with a national labor organization that has become a very conservative and highly bureaucratized institution, defending the *status quo* which is now directly attacked by the Negro in virtually every area of American life.

Many trade unions lag behind the progress made by other institutions in the community. In East St. Louis, Illinois, and Tulsa, Oklahoma, for example, Negro children attend integrated schools during the day, but their parents attend segregated union meetings at night, if they are admitted into labor unions at all. . . .

There is a deep distrust among many Negro wage earners and others within the Negro community toward trade unions. It is a distrust well founded in experience. For today, as in the past, there is a profound disparity between the public image presented by the national AFL-CIO and the day-to-day realities as experienced by many Negro workers. This is true in the North as well as the South. There are a few exceptions, especially in the mass production industries where, historically, there has been a large concentration of Negro workers and in some unions such as the United Automobile Workers (UAW), the United Packinghouse Workers (UPW), and the National Maritime Union (NMU) where there is an ideological sensitivity to the "Negro question."

But for the Negro in major areas of the economy, in the building and construction trades, in the railroad industry, among the Seafarers and the Boilermakers and the oil and chemical workers and machinists, in pulp, tobacco, and paper manufacturing, in metal working, in the printing trades, and in many other industries highly unionized for a long period of time, trade union practices are characterized by a broad pattern of discrimination and segregation.

AFL-CIO affiliated unions engage in four basic categories of discriminatory racial practices. They are: exclusion of Negroes from membership, segregated locals, separate seniority lines in collective bargaining agreements, and refusal to admit qualified Negroes into apprenticeship training programs controlled by unions.

❊   ❊   ❊

The United Brotherhood of Carpenters and Joiners, for over a half-century, has been among the most important of all the building trades unions, and, with very few exceptions, organizes Negroes and whites into separate locals insofar as it permits Negroes to join the union at all. In the South there seems to be no exception to this rule, and it is most often followed in Northern cities as well. . . .

The white locals are in control of the union hiring hall, and, because of frequent arrangements with municipal and county political machines, all hiring for major public as well as private construction projects is done through the "lily-white" union hiring hall. Quite frequently Negroes are excluded altogether from work in white neighborhoods. This means that Negro carpenters are restricted to marginal maintenance and repair work within the Negro community and that they seldom are permitted to work on the larger construction projects. The same practices are true for other building-trades unions in many cities throughout the country.

* * *

On occasion one or two Negroes have been admitted into an all-white local union as token compliance within a state or municipal fair employment practice law, as with the International Brotherhood of Electrical Workers in Cleveland, the Bricklayers Union in Milwaukee, and the Railway Clerks Union in Minneapolis, but this is essentially a limited and strategic adjustment to community pressure and represents very dubious "progress."

Certainly the token admission of a few Negroes into an electrical workers union in Cleveland or Washington, D.C. can no more be regarded as integration than can the token admission of two or three Negro children into a Southern public school. There are also several instances where unions have removed the "lily-white" exclusion clause from their constitutions as public relations gestures only, but continue to exclude Negroes from membership by tacit consent.

As long as union membership remains a condition of employment in many trades and crafts and Negroes are barred from union membership solely because of their color, then trade union discrimination is the decisive factor in determining whether Negro workers in a given industry shall have an opportunity to earn a living for themselves and their families. This is especially true in the printing trades, the construction industry, and other occupations where labor unions exercise a high degree of control over access to employment.

* * *

Negroes may be winning the broad legal and social struggles for equality in the United States, but they are losing the battle for equal employment opportunity and economic justice. At the present time, the historic civil rights gains won by Negroes in the past twenty years are in danger of being destroyed by the growing crisis of unemployment and underemployment that directly affects the well-being of the entire Negro community and leads to acute social dislocation and despair.

NOTES

1. U.S. Commission on Civil Rights, *Employment, 1961*, Report No. 3, pp. 65–66.
2. Donald Dewey, "Negro Employment in Southern Industry," *Journal of Political Economy*, LX (August 1952), 279–293.
3. *Equal Protection of the Laws in North Carolina: Report of the North Carolina Advisory Committee to the United States Commission on Civil Rights*, 1962, Washington, D.C., p. 87.
4. New York State Commission Against Discrimination, *Apprentices, Skilled Craftsmen and the Negro: An Analysis* (New York, 1960); Herbert Hill, *The Negro Wage-Earner and Apprenticeship Training Programs* (New York: National Association for the Advancement of Colored People, 1960).
5. See *Congressional Record—House*, January 31, 1963, pp. 1496–1499 (Testimony of Herbert Hill on Racial Practices of ILGWU). See also Herbert Hill, "The ILGWU—Fact and Fiction," *New Politics*, 1962, No. 2, pp. 7–27.

THE NEGRO IN THE NATIONAL ECONOMY

Andrew F. Brimmer

In analyzing the experience of the black entrepreneur in recent years, Andrew F. Brimmer found evidence of the heavy dependence of Negro businessmen on the segregated Negro market. The competition of white firms tends to be quite strong when blacks have relatively free access to goods and services in the general marketplace. By implication, this raises serious questions about the potentiality of black capitalism, at least insofar as it is interpreted as Negro entrepreneurship in the ghetto. Dr. Brimmer is a Governor of the Federal Reserve System.

NEGROES AS ENTREPRENEURS

Trends in General Business

. . . Segregation has served the Negro businessman in the same way a tariff protects an infant industry. With the removal or reduction of a tariff wall, major adjustments must be made by those who have benefited from its existence. The Negro businessman is faced with such an adjustment. As the process of desegregation permeates the marketplace, Negro-owned businesses (the vast majority of which concentrate on providing personal services in a segregated market) are faced with increased competition from firms catering to buyers with a decreasing reference to race.

The consequences of this process are already evident. Because we have only fragmentary statistics on Negro-owned business, it is difficult to chart these trends with precision. However, since the vast majority of Negro businesses are single proprietorships—rather than partner-

From "The Negro in the National Economy," by Andrew F. Brimmer. Excerpted and reprinted from *The American Negro Reference Book*, ed. John P. Davis (Englewood Cliffs, N.J.: Prentice-Hall, 1966) by permission of Prentice-Hall, Inc., and Andrew F. Brimmer. Copyright © 1966 by Prentice-Hall, Inc.

ships or corporations—Bureau of the Census statistics on self-employed managers, proprietors and officials give a fair indication of the scope of Negro business. . . .

Even a cursory analysis of the evidence clearly demonstrates the heavy dependence of Negro businessmen on the segregated Negro market. Where Negro customers have relatively free access to goods and services sold in the general marketplace, Negro businessmen have made little headway against the strong competition of white firms. In 1960, Negroes constituted about 2.5 per cent of all self-employed businessmen, but this ratio varied greatly among different industries. Their largest share of a major industry was personal services (3.4 per cent); at the bottom of the spectrum was banking and finance, where Negroes represented less than two-tenths of one per cent of the total. But behind the array of ratios is an interesting and significant story. If we divide the retail trade sector according to the principal types of stores, we see immediately the importance of segregation in providing opportunities for Negro entrepreneurs. For example, in 1960, Negroes operated 2.6 per cent of all retail outlets—but 5.6 per cent of the eating and drinking establishments. They also had 4.1 per cent of the food stores; this is a reflection of the fact that such stores (especially smaller ones) are typically located in or near segregated residential areas.

In sharp contrast, Negroes owned much less than one per cent of the retail establishments selling apparel, furniture, hardware or motor vehicles. In these categories, the meager ownership role played by Negroes can be attributed partly to the fact that few of them can obtain the relatively large amount of capital required for successful operation. Another factor appears to be the sizable volume of sales necessary to sustain such a business. However, the most basic explanation seems to be the freedom Negro customers have to shop for these items in stores catering to the general market. The slightly stronger position of Negroes as operators of gasoline stations is due primarily to the vigorous and competitive efforts of the leading petroleum companies to establish franchise outlets in or near the geographical areas occupied by Negroes in the key population centers. Outside of retail trade, the provision of personal services to Negro customers has been a mainstay of Negro businessmen. The most outstanding examples are owners of barbershops and beauty salons. In fact, this area alone has generated a complex of interrelated activities by Negro businessmen. . . . For instance, the majority of the 1,300 Negroes who owned manufacturing firms in 1960 were probably producing cosmetics and barber and beauty shop supplies especially for the Negro trade. Undoubtedly, a fairly large proportion of the 2,600 Negro businessmen engaged in wholesale trade were distributing these items to local shops. Still other businessmen (e.g., insurance and real estate brokers, and those providing a variety of business services) were probably only slightly less dependent on the segregated Negro market. On the other hand, Negroes owning automotive repair facilities, running transportation (such as taxis and local haulage), and doing construction jobs normally would find their customers in the community at large—although Negro customers may provide their ultimate base of support.

But this configuration of Negro-owned businesses is changing drastically as Negro consumers are increasingly attracted to the general market. Between 1950 and 1960, the total number of Negro businessmen shrank by more than one-fifth. While there was a similar decrease in the total number of self-employed businessmen during the decade, the proportion was smaller. Moreover, much of the decline in the overall number was accounted for by the change to the corporate form of organization. This was much less true for Negroes.

Furthermore, with few exceptions, the incidence of decline was greater for Negroes, compared with the total, in those fields where segregation and discrimination imposed the least constraints on Negro customers. For instance, the annual average percentage changes between 1950 and 1960 in several key areas for Negroes and the total self-employed, respectively were: communications, utilities and sanitary services, −11.2 vs. −1.2; transportation, −6.5 vs. −2.9; furniture and housefurnishing, −6.1 vs. −2.9; apparel and accessories, −5.9 vs. −3.6; hardware and building materials, −3.9 vs. −1.6. It is difficult to account for the causes underlying these specific decreases, but several considerations can be cited. The sharp drop in the number of Negroes in the private sanitary services (and the growth in the total number of businessmen engaged in this activity) probably reflects the increased competition from large firms which move trash for restaurants, department stores and similar establishments on a contract basis. A similar explanation probably applies in the case of transportation. In the past, numerous small Negro businesses were formed around one or two trucks, with the owner and a few helpers providing local moving and job-by-job transportation services. However, with the growing unionization of the trucking industry, even extending into purely local transportation, the rising wage levels have made such opportunities increasingly attractive to white men. The trend toward the use of more sophisticated equipment (such as refrigerator trucks and other specialty vehicles) has also necessitated the accumulation of considerably more capital than most Negro truckers could raise. In addition, the number of Negro taxi owners in the major cities (with the possible exception of Washington, D.C.) has shrunk as gigantic corporations have acquired franchises to operate fleets of several thousand vehicles. The decline in the retail outlets undoubtedly reflects the diffusion of mass marketing throughout the economy; this has made it exceedingly difficult for the small Negro retailer (along with similarly situated white merchants) to compete with the super-market, large department stores and discount houses.

Several other types of traditional Negro businesses, . . . also experienced absolute decline or a severe slackening in the rate of growth. For example, the number of funeral directors dropped by 6 per cent between 1950 and 1960, and the number of barbers decreased by over 16 per cent. While the number of Negro-owned hotels and motels has continued to expand, they have lost a sizable proportion of their most desirable clientele—a loss only partly made up by the growth of luxury and semiluxury resort and vacation sites.

On the other hand, Negro businessmen made significant strides in several new or revitalized fields. The number of self-employed in construction climbed by more than 17 per cent, about the same rate achieved by this category as a whole. Substantial gains were also registered in the ownership of gasoline service stations, automotive repair shops and garages. In manufacturing, modest expansion occurred. This gain was made despite the capture by large corporations of a fairly sizable share of the cosmetics market among Negro customers, which traditionally accounted for virtually all of the output of Negro manufacturing firms. Many of the more recent ventures in manufacturing include plastics, apparel, food processing and other relatively new areas.

In analyzing these general trends in Negro-owned businesses during the last decade or so, the intention is not to paint a bleak picture of total stagnation and decline. On the contrary, a great number of individual Negro businesses have been launched and have achieved considerable success. Moreover, many established firms have made substantial progress. Indeed, without much difficulty, one can find exceptionally prosperous businessmen whose enterprises stand out against the general trend in any of the areas described here. Nevertheless, when the basic trends are viewed against the panorama of the overall business landscape, one cannot escape concluding that Negro businessmen taken as a group have lost considerable ground and are facing an uncertain future.

Trends in the earnings of Negro businessmen also support this general conclusion. Again the historical paradox of segregation as a protective shield is evident: nonwhite businessmen concentrating in the segregated market tend to earn relatively more, compared with all self-employed entrepreneurs, than their colleagues competing in the open market. For example, in 1949, the median income of nonwhite professional workers taken as a group was $2,269, about 58 per cent of the median income of all professionals ($3,949). Among salaried managerial personnel, total and nonwhite median incomes were $4,403 and $2,134, respectively, yielding a ratio of 49 per cent. Among self-employed businessmen, the income figures were: total, $3,502 and nonwhite, $1,860, for a ratio of 53 per cent. But nonwhites providing personal services to a segregated market (barbers, beauticians, etc.) had a median income of $2,174 in 1949, equal to 70 per cent of that earned by all those offering personal services. For operators of retail food stores in predominantly Negro neighborhoods, the ratio was 63 per cent, and for nonwhite restaurant owners it was 60 per cent. By 1959 virtually all of these proportions had risen. However, the extra advantage derived by Negro businessmen from the segregated market was still visible. The ratio of nonwhite to total median income of self-employed owners was 56 per cent; it was 78 per cent for food outlets and about 65 per cent for personal services and eating and drinking places. In contrast, in the more open manufacturing and transportation sectors, the proportions were much smaller—44 per cent and 42 per cent, respectively.

In interpreting the above figures, however, the reader should not conclude that self-employment is an easy way for Negroes to become rich. In fact, one can infer that the financial return to Negro risk-takers in general is probably substantially less than for the total population when appraised in terms of alternative opportunities. Yet, the gap appears to be smaller for nonwhite businessmen than for professionals. For instance, in 1959 self-employed nonwhites had a median income of 73 per cent of that for all nonwhite professional workers. The comparable figure for all self-employed was 87 per cent. Expressed differently, the typical nonwhite businessman in 1959 earned about $65 per week, while the average nonwhite professional worker earned approximately $90 per week. Among the total population the corresponding figures were $114 and $130, respectively. Once these figures are adjusted to reflect what Negro businessmen typically bring to their enterprises, the discrepancy seems to disappear. Of course, nothing is known about the amount of capital invested by either group of businessmen or professionals. Consequently, it is impossible to estimate the profitability of either type of activity; to do this figures on rate of return would be needed. However, the information available on educational attainment suggests that Negro businessmen do seem to enjoy a higher income per year of schooling than do Negro professionals. Self-employed nonwhite businessmen (with an average of 9.0 years of school completed) have just over half as much education as nonwhite professionals (with 16.3 years of schooling). In contrast, the comparable educational attainment for all self-employed businessmen was nearly three-quarters of that for all professionals—12.1 years and 16.3 years. Nevertheless, the median income of the nonwhite business group in 1959 was in the neighborhood of three-quarters of that for nonwhite professionals. Thus, there is a strong suggestion that part of the income of Negro businessmen is a reflection—not exclusively of their investment in capital and education—but also is a reflection of the partial protection afforded by a segregated market.

Banking and Finance

Even a cursory look makes it evident that Negroes cast a pale shadow on the financial landscape. At the end of 1963, Negroes owned or controlled thirteen banks and about fifty life insurance companies. They also had thirty-four Federally-insured savings and loan associations, of which twenty had charters granted by the Federal Government. The combined assets of these three groups of financial institutions amounted to $764 million, or only 0.12 per cent of the total assets held by similar financial enterprises in the country as a whole. While a number of the individual businesses have been strikingly successful, their collective impact has been insignificant.

This indifferent progress cannot be attributed to the reluctance of Negroes to venture onto the financial terrain. Indeed, even before the Civil War, Negroes made numerous attempts to launch banks. The Freedmen's Savings Bank and Trust Company, sponsored by the Freedmen's Bureau, was the most ambitious effort. In its heyday, it had a network of branches in thirty-six cities, and its deposits reached a peak of $57 million. While the bulk of its deposits was backed by United States Government bonds, its reserve funds apparently were not managed well. In any case, the failure of the bank in the depression of 1874 greatly damaged the confidence of Negro depositors in Negro-owned institutions.* Yet, during each subsequent period of sustained prosperity, a new crop of Negro banks appeared. But again and again, the end of prosperity brought another epidemic of bank failures and widespread losses to depositors. While this pattern was also typical of the behavior of the banking system as a whole, the legacy in the poverty-stricken Negro community was particularly discouraging.

Among Negro-owned insurance companies, the record is somewhat better. The primary explanation, of course, is the protection provided by the discriminatory practices of the principal insurance companies serving the community at large.

✸   ✸   ✸

Negro-Owned Banks

. . . The combined resources of the thirteen Negro banks amounted to about $77 million at the end of 1963, compared with $364 billion of

---

* Gunnar Myrdal, *An American Dilemma* (New York: Harper & Bros., 1944), Vol. I, p. 314.

total assets held by the 14,079 banks in the country as a whole. Thus, Negro banks represented only 0.021 per cent of the nation's banking business. But even this small figure reflected an improvement, because in 1957, their share was 0.018 per cent. In the intervening years, the Negro banks as a group experienced an annual average rate of growth of 8.6 per cent, compared with 5.9 per cent for all banks in the nation. While the Negro banks' faster expansion partly reflected their small size (thus permitting even a modest absolute gain to be registered as a large percentage), much of their progress was genuine. Moreover, in 1964 six Negro banks received charters or actually opened for business, and three others were seeking charters. All except two of these new institutions were national banks, reflecting a substantial liberalization of policy by Federal banking officials. Nevertheless, Negro banks remain modest institutions.

✻   ✻   ✻

Negro-Owned Life Insurance Companies

The field of life insurance provides a classic illustration of the origins and rationale of Negro business: the exclusive and discriminating practices of the companies serving the national market created a protected environment in which the Negro institutions could develop. Beginning in the 1880's, most of the leading insurance firms began to employ a separate mortality table to estimate risks of insuring Negro lives; this separate table resulted in substantially higher premiums for Negroes for the same amount of coverage. Still other companies refused to insure Negroes under any circumstances. Since many Negroes, along with other citizens, foresaw the desirability of insurance coverage, the conditions were set for the growth of Negro life insurance companies. While the record is replete with numerous failures (which is also true of white-owned and controlled companies), the life insurance field remains the outstanding example of Negro enterprise.

At the end of 1963, Negroes owned some fifty-odd legal reserve life insurance companies. They also maintained more than thirty burial and mutual aid societies. All of the latter are small, localized ventures, with a total of only $1 million of assets in 1962. Moreover, accurate statistics are available for only the twenty or so largest companies which hold virtually all of the assets owned by Negro institutions. . . .

. . . The twenty leading Negro companies had total assets of $311 million in 1962. This represented about 0.23 per cent of the $133 billion of total assets owned by all life insurance companies. Thus, compared with Negro-owned banks (which held only 0.021 per cent

of total banking assets at the end of 1963), the relative position of
the Negro insurance companies in the financial community is con-
siderably stronger. . . .

The Future of Negroes in Business

If the fields in which Negro businessmen have traditionally con-
centrated are less promising than in the past, what alternative oppor-
tunities are likely to appear in the future? For Negroes, as for other
citizens in the business world, such opportunities are likely to be
found primarily as managers and officials employed by our medium
and large corporations and public enterprises. That Negroes have
made little progress in this field is common knowledge. For example,
in 1960, about 8 per cent of the total civilian labor force of 68 million
was engaged as nonfarm managers, officials and proprietors. Less
than 1.5 per cent of the 6.6 million Negroes in the labor force were
so engaged. If the percentages had been approximately equal, there
would have been about 525 thousand—rather than the actual 191
thousand—Negroes in the managerial class. Furthermore, over half
of the Negro managerial group was self-employed, compared with
just over one-third of all managers in the country.

*   *   *

Thus, from these data a clear inference can be drawn: with a change
in aspriations among potential Negro businessmen, better preparation
on their part and a genuine commitment to equal opportunity by
leaders in the corporate business community, the future could be
promising for a number of Negro businessmen.

Some progress is already being made in this direction, although few
corporate executives would claim that the pace has been rapid. A
rough indication of the current trends is given by the experience of
those companies which participate in "Plans for Progress." This is a
voluntary program to expand access to jobs, operated in conjunction
with the President's Committee on Equal Opportunity. In a report
covering the period when the companies joined Plans for Progress
through mid-July, 1964, 103 of these firms reported that their total
employment increased by 300,796 or 7.6 per cent. Just over two-fifths
of this gain represented an expansion in white collar employment.
During the same period, these companies added 40,938 employees
from minority groups. This represented about 13.6 per cent of the
expansion in total employment. On the other hand, nonwhites filled
about 11.0 per cent of the increase in white collar jobs.

When these companies joined Plans for Progress, nonwhites con-
stituted about 5 per cent of their total labor force, and they represented
approximately 1.2 per cent of those in the managerial group. In the

subsequent expansion in employment, nonwhites obtained about 3,000 (or 2 per cent) of the new jobs in the management category. While this gain is obviously very small, it does represent about 1,000 more managerial and technical positions for nonwhites than might have been expected on the basis of the companies' traditional employment practice.

Simultaneously, many corporations are making a special effort to recruit and train Negroes and other minority group citizens for corporate positions. Some of this effort undoubtedly can be written off as "image-making" by some firms, who would like to point to their recruiting efforts which have—unfortunately—failed to produce "qualified" candidates. On the whole, however, the vast majority of corporate recruiters seem to be making a genuine effort to identify and to enroll promising minority group candidates. On the other hand, given the criteria which the typical corporation uses in selecting its managerial personnel, most corporate recruiters are undoubtedly finding it difficult to locate qualified personnel. The sources of these difficulties are widely known. They spring from the vicious circle created by a history of discriminatory employment practices; poor undergraduate training provided by the archaic curricula of basically segregated institutions attended by many Negro college students; a resulting peculiar pattern of occupational preferences stressing medicine, law, teaching and the ministry; a reluctance to venture into the expanding fields of business administration and related social sciences, engineering and other technical areas—which result in only marginal preparation for management careers in business.

✽   ✽   ✽

Future Opportunities for Ownership

Of course, the chance to go into business for themselves is an option which will remain open to Negroes along with other citizens. However, before this option is taken up in the future, potential Negro business should give careful consideration to several factors that are rapidly reshaping the environment in which they will have to operate. While the majority of Negro businessmen are correct in assuming that (within the foreseeable future) they will have to rely primarily on Negro customers for their patronage, they apparently do not realize that in the future they will have to compete in a wholly different type of market. As mentioned above, the desegregation of places of public accommodation, such as restaurants, theaters, hotels and similar establishments, will have a serious impact on many of the sheltered businesses which most Negro businessmen have operated behind the barriers induced by segregation. With greater access to facilities pro-

vided for the public in general, Negro customers will increasingly de-
mand that Negro businesses compete in terms of quality of services
provided at competitive prices.

Further, there is a prime need to shift from the single proprietorship
form of organization, which is so dominant among Negro businessmen,
to the corporate form which is the key to financing business expansion.
The superiority of the corporation over unincorporated enterprises as
a medium for expanding business has been clearly demonstrated, and
growth as opposed to stagnation has always been a measure of busi-
ness health. Recent data on the distribution of firms by type of organi-
zation and the relative share of receipts and profits show that
relatively few companies account for the major share of the nation's
business, and these are the large and ever-growing corporations. For
example, in 1960, corporations constituted about 10 per cent of the
total number of businesses in existence. However, the total receipts
of corporations were $803 billion, representing over three-quarters of
the total. Their net profits, after allowing for losses amounted to $44
billion, or three-fifths of the total net profits of business enterprises.

But whatever form of organization a businessman chooses for his
operation, several conditions must be met if success is to be realized.
In the first instance, a businessman must perceive a market for a
product or service. Next, steps must be taken to translate this idea
into a practicable production process. Thirdly, technical and man-
agerial know-how must be sufficient to establish and conduct an
enterprise. Financial resources, especially equity capital, must be avail-
able or acquired. A skilled labor force must exist or must be trained.
Finally, the businessman must possess enough marketing know-how
to find and maintain customers in the face of competition from other
products and services. As we all know, the typical Negro-owned firm
is deficient in all or most of these vital requirements.

While there is no shortage of potential Negro businessmen, there is
a severe shortage of technical know-how outside the traditional areas
of trade and personal services. This lack of mastery over technical
requirements may well be an obstacle as great as the lack of equity
capital. . . .

The above observations focus on only a few of the growing op-
portunities for Negro businessmen to participate in the future growth
of the country. Above all, there will undoubtedly be a variety of
ventures engaged in the production and distribution of goods and
services for the community as a whole. Moreover, there will un-
doubtedly be growing opportunities for Negroes to participate in the
management activities of large corporations which are also oriented
to the general market. It should be emphasized again that desegrega-
tion of the marketplace which is already well under way will require
desegregation in the ownership and management of business enter-

prises as well. While the future of a segregated Negro-owned business, existing in a segregated market, appears not to be bright, the future of Negroes in the business life of the country in general does appear to be more promising than ever before.

PART III

The Housing Market

THE NEGRO AS AN IMMIGRANT GROUP: RECENT TRENDS IN RACIAL AND ETHNIC SEGREGATION IN CHICAGO

Karl E. Taeuber
Alma F. Taeuber

The large-scale migration of Negroes to large northern cities has been compared to the immigration of millions of Europeans during the last half of the nineteenth and the first two decades of the twentieth century. Unlike the European populations who assimilated into the economy and the social structure of American society, the Negroes have persisted as a disadvantaged and residentially segregated group. Karl and Alma Taeuber use data for Chicago to analyze recent trends in racial and ethnic segregation and to determine whether it is useful to view the Negro population as an immigrant population. Karl Taeuber is a Professor of Sociology at the University of Wisconsin and on the research staff of the University's Institute for Research on Poverty. Alma Taeuber is a Research Associate at the Institute for Research on Poverty.

During the last half of the nineteenth century and the early decades of the twentieth, millions of immigrants from Europe entered the United States. Many of these immigrants settled initially in ethnic colonies in large northern cities and found jobs as unskilled laborers in burgeoning mass-production industries. With the onset of World War I in Europe, and with the passage of restrictive legislation in the

United States in the early 1920's, the period of massive overseas migration came to an end. At the same time, however, there developed a large-scale migration of Negroes from the South to the same large northern industrial cities. Like the immigrants from abroad, the Negro migrants to northern cities filled the lowest occupational niches and rapidly developed highly segregated patterns of residence within the central cities.

In view of many obvious similarities between the Negro migrants and the various immigrant groups preceding them, it has been suggested that northern urban Negroes are but the latest of the immigrant groups, undergoing much the same processes of adaptation to city life and of assimilation into the general social structure as the European groups preceding them. The persistence of Negroes as a residentially segregated and underprivileged group at the lowest levels of socioeconomic status, however, is frequently interpreted in terms of distinctive aspects of the Negro experience, particularly their historical position in American society.

The question of whether or not a northern urban Negro population can fruitfully be viewed as an immigrant population, comparable to European immigrant populations of earlier decades with respect to the nature and speed of assimilation, will be explored on the basis of data permitting analysis of recent trends in racial and ethnic segregation in Chicago.

*   *   *

For our purposes, it will suffice to have a working definition of the process of assimilation considerably less sophisticated than that required for a general sociological theory. Accepting the view that both immigrant groups and Negro migrants originally settled in segregated patterns in central areas of cities and ranked very low in terms of socioeconomic measures, assimilation then consisted in large part of a process of social and economic advancement on the part of the original members of the group and their descendants, along with a decreasing residential concentration in ethnic colonies. . . .

The data in Table 1 illustrate for selected immigrant groups the patterns of socioeconomic advance and residential dispersion from highly segregated ethnic colonies. For each of the larger ethnic groups, data for 1950 show the average standing on three measures of socioeconomic status, standardized for age, of the first generation (the foreign-born white, FBW) and the second generation (native white of foreign or mixed parentage, NWFMP). The nationality groups are split into "old," "new," and "newer" groups in an extension of the traditional system. On the average, comparing within the first or within the second generation, the "old" immigrant groups are the best off on these measures, the "new" groups are intermediate, and

the "newer" groups are the worst off. It cannot be determined from
these data to what extent the old immigrants are better off by virtue
of their longer average length of residence in the United States, or to
what extent they may have been better off at their time of immigration
than the newer immigrants were at the time of their move.

*   *   *

Measures of the changing residential patterns of the immigrant groups
are given in columns 7–9 of Table 1. The measure, an index of resi-
dential segregation between the total foreign stock (FBW + NWFMP)
of each nationality and the total native whites of native parentage
(NWNP), assumes a value of 100 for maximum residential segregation
and a value of 0 if the residential distributions are identical. The
indexes were computed from the distribution of each group among
the seventy-five community areas of the city of Chicago for 1930
(the last previous census year that included information on the total
foreign stock) and 1960. The degree of residential segregation from
the native population is highest for the "newer" immigrants and lowest
for the "old" immigrants. Between 1930 and 1960, most of the ethnic
groups became less segregated from the native population. Only for
England, Ireland, and Sweden did the indexes fail to decline, and
these were already at relatively low levels.[1]

This general approach to the measurement or assimilation of immi-
grant groups has been pursued for a number of cities and longer time
periods by Lieberson. He found a remarkably persistent and consist-
ent association through time between residential desegregation of an
ethnic group and increasing socioeconomic similarity to native whites,
and cross-sectionally between the position of each group as compared
to others on measures of residential segregation and its relative levels
on status measures.[2]

The index of residential segregation between Negroes and NWNP
for 1930 was 84, and for 1960, 82. These values are higher than any
of those for specific immigrant stocks. Furthermore, each of the immi-
grant stocks was highly segregated from Negroes in 1930 and 1960.
There is relatively little intermixture of Negro residences with those
of any group of whites. Even the "newer" immigrant groups, the
Puerto Ricans and Mexicans, are not joining or replacing Negroes in
established Negro areas but are moving into separate ethnic colonies
of their own at the periphery of Negro areas. Negroes clearly occupy
a distinctive position as the most residentially segregated of the
principal migrant groups. The separation of Negroes from all groups
of whites is sharper than any of the patterns of residential segregation
between ethnic groups or between socioeconomic groups within the
white population.[3] Apparently this pattern has developed during the
last few decades. Lieberson has demonstrated that, although prior to

the great Negro migrations of World War I there were instances of immigrant stocks being more segregated from native whites than were Negroes, since 1920 there has been a general tendency for Negro residential segregation to be highest.[4]

Data pertaining specifically to the comparison between whites and non-whites (97 per cent of Chicago's non-whites are Negroes) on measures of socioeconomic status and of residential segregation are presented in Table 2. For each of four measures reflecting socioeconomic status, there was improvement in the status of the non-white population between 1940 and 1960. (For whites, improving status would be more clearly evident if the data referred to the entire metropolitan area rather than just the city of Chicago.) The indexes of residential segregation between whites and Negroes, in the top panel of the table, show minor fluctuations around an extremely high level and give no indication of the decline anticipated on the basis of the socioeconomic advancement of the Negro population. That this is not an atypical finding is indicated by reference to other data showing a long term historical trend toward increasing residential segregation between whites and non-whites. Increasing racial residential segregation was evident in most large cities of the United States between 1940 and 1950, while during the 1950's, southern cities continued to increase in segregation and northern cities generally registered modest declines.[5]

In broad perspective, the historical trend toward improving socioeconomic status of immigrant groups has gone hand in hand with decreasing residential segregation. In contrast, Negro residential segregation from whites has increased steadily over past decades until it has reached universally high levels in cities throughout the United States, despite advances in the socioeconomic status of Negroes.

*   *   *

Decreasing residential concentration of immigrant groups occurred despite the efforts of many nationality organizations to maintain the ethnic colonies.[6] Few Negro organizations have been as explicitly segregationist. In some immigrant groups, many members were dispersing from the ethnic colonies even while large-scale immigration of that group was still under way. For every immigrant group, diminishing residential segregation has been evident since the cessation of large-scale immigration. For Negroes, however, residential segregation has increased since the first period of large-scale immigration to northern cities, and this increase in residential segregation continued during the late 1920's and 1930's when the volume of migration was at a low level. These observations tend to discredit the argument that a major barrier to residential dispersal of the Negro population of Chicago is its continuing rapid increase. However, the size of the

TABLE 1

Selected Characteristics (Age-Standardized) of Foreign-Born and Native Ethnic Populations in 1950, and Indexes of Residential Segregation of Selected Groups of Foreign Stock from Native Whites of Native Parentage, 1930 and 1960, Chicago*

Country of Origin	Per Cent High-School Graduates (Males Age 25 and Over)		Per Cent with Income above $3,000 (Persons with Income)		Per Cent with White-Collar Jobs (Employed Males)		Index of Residential Segregation (Compared with NWNP)		
	FBW	NWFMP	FBW	NWFMP	FBW	NWFMP	1930	1960	Change
"Old" immigrant groups:									
England and Wales	45	50	53	58	49	51	11	18	+ 7
Ireland	24	47	47	56	22	47	23	31	+ 8
Norway	31	47	54	57	24	51	44	37	− 7
Sweden	25	48	59	60	23	51	26	30	+ 4
Germany	37	34	53	55	34	42	22	19	− 3
"New" immigrant groups:									
Austria	29	40	54	57	33	44	30	16	−14
Czechoslovakia	25	33	44	54	22	36	59	37	−22
Italy	15	27	47	53	24	37	52	32	−20
Poland	18	25	42	49	25	30	63	38	−25
U.S.S.R.	35	60	60	69	59	74	51	44	− 7

"Newer" immigrant groups								
Mexico	14	16	38	29	8	13	71	54	−17
Puerto Rico†	13	29	16	37	22	36	†	67	†

* Data for 1930 and 1950 refer to foreign white stock (foreign-born plus native of foreign or mixed parentage); data for 1960 refer to total foreign stock. Abbreviations used are FBW for foreign-born white, NWFMP for native white of foreign or mixed parentage, and NWNP for native white of native parentage. The three socioeconomic characteristics refer to the Standard Metropolitan Area population, while the segregation indexes are based on community areas within the city. Age-standardization was by the direct method, using age groups 25–44 and 45 and over, with the Standard Metropolitan Area age composition as a standard.

† Socioeconomic characteristics for Puerto Rican population refer to total United States; Puerto Rican population by community areas for Chicago available for 1960 only.

Source: Characteristics from U.S. Bureau of the Census, *U.S. Census of Population: 1950*, Vol. IV, *Special Reports*, Pt. 3, chap. A, "Nativity and Parentage," and chap. D, "Puerto Ricans in Continental United States." Distributions of population by community areas for 1930 and 1960 from data on file at Chicago Community Inventory, University of Chicago.

TABLE 2

Selected Socioeconomic Characteristics (Unstandardized) of Whites and Non-Whites, Chicago, 1940, 1950, and 1960

Characteristic	Non-white	White
Residential segregation index, whites vs. Negroes:*		
1930	85	
1940	85	
1950	79	
1960	83	
Per cent high school graduates, ages 25+:		
1940	16	25
1950	25	37
1960	29	37
Per cent white collar, male:		
1940	17	40
1950	17	41
1960	21	40
Per cent home-owners:		
1940	7	26
1950	12	33
1960	16	39
Per cent multiple-person households with 1.01 or more persons per room:		
1940	41	17
1950	46	14
1960	34	10

* These values differ slightly from those cited in the text for Negroes as compared to native whites of native parentage.

Source: Data for 1940 from the 1940 Census Tract Bulletin for Chicago; for 1950 from Philip M. Hauser and Evelyn M. Kitagawa (eds.), *Local Community Fact Book for Chicago, 1950* (Chicago: Chicago Community Inventory, 1953); and for 1960 from the 1960 Census Tract Bulletin for Chicago.

Negro population and the magnitude of its annual increase are larger than for any single ethnic group in the past, and comparisons with smaller groups are not completely convincing. That rapid increase of Negro population does not necessarily lead to increasing residential segregation was demonstrated directly in the intercity comparative study previously cited. There was no definite relationship between increase in Negro population and increase in the value of the segregation index. Indeed, during the 1950–60 decade, there appeared to be a slight relationship in the opposite direction.[7]

❋   ❋   ❋

It has been suggested that considerable time is required for Negroes to make the transition from a "primitive folk culture" to "urbanism as a way of life." [8] Several types of data indicate that large and increasing proportions of the Negro urban population are city-born and raised.

*　　*　　*

The "visibility" of Negroes due to skin color and other features which make the large majority of second-, third-, and later-generation descendants readily identifiable as Negroes is often cited as a basic factor in accounting for the distinctive position of Negroes in our society. It is exceedingly difficult to assess the significance of visibility. There is no other group that is strictly comparable to Negroes regarding every factor except visibility. It is not completely irrelevant, however, to note that non-white skin color, by itself, is not an insurmountable handicap in our society. The socioeconomic status of the Japanese population of Chicago in 1950 substantially exceeded that of the Negro population; and their residential segregation from whites, although high, was considerably lower than that between Negroes and whites.[9] Unfortunately there are no trend data available on the characteristics of the Japanese in Chicago. A more appropriate Japanese population for comparison, however, is the much larger one in the San Francisco area. A recent study there affirmed that "ethnic colonies of Japanese are gone or rapidly going" and documented their rapid socioeconomic advance.[10]

In the traditional immigrant pattern, the more recent immigrants displaced the older groups at the bottom socioeconomic levels. How do the Negroes compare with the other "newer" immigrant groups, the Mexicans and the Puerto Ricans? The limited data now available suggest that the Negroes may soon be left alone at the bottom of the social and economic scale. We have already noted (from data in Table 1) that the "newer" groups were, in 1950, of very low status compared to the other immigrant groups, and that their residential segregation from the native whites of native percentage was the highest of all the immigrant groups. For 1960, data on distribution within Chicago of persons born in Puerto Rico are available separately from data on those persons born in the United States of Puerto Rican parentage. Thus it is possible to compute indexes of residential segregation for first- and second-generation Puerto Ricans. For Chicago in 1960, these index values were 68.4 for the first generation and 64.9 for the second generation, indicating that residential dispersion has already begun for the Puerto Ricans. This difference actually understates the amount of dispersion, since the second generation consists in large proportion of children still living with their first-generation parents.

Selected socioeconomic measures for the Puerto Rican and the non-white populations of Chicago in 1960 are shown in Table 3. On every measure, the Puerto Rican population is less well off—it is less educated, has lower income, is more crowded, is less likely to own homes, is less well housed, and lives in older buildings. Yet the index of residential segregation (computed with respect to NWNP) for Puerto Ricans is 67 as compared with 82 for Negroes.

Up to now we have been making comparisons between Negroes and immigrant groups, demonstrating that residential dispersion has not accompanied socioeconomic advance by Negroes in the way that it did for immigrant groups. Economic status and expenditure for housing, however, are clearly correlated, and there is also a correlation between economic status and residential segregation. By virtue of variations in the type, age, and quality of housing, and in the patterns of residential choice by persons of varying socioeconomic status, the subareas of a city are differentiated in terms of the average status of their residents. Since Negroes are of much lower average status than whites, they would be expected to be disproportionately represented in low-status residential areas. In fact, an extreme position regarding the relationships between patterns of socioeconomic residential segregation and racial residential segregation would attribute all of the latter to the former. Such a position is sometimes offered as a counter-argument to charges of racial discrimination against the real estate business. To the extent that this position is correct, it might be expected that future economic advances on the part of the Negro population should be translated into decreased residential segregation.

The task of partialing out a component of racial segregation due to economic factors involves some difficult methodological problems, and no method is entirely satisfactory.[11] Our approach utilizes indirect standardization of available census data. Let us delineate the status of a residential area in terms of, say, the income distribution of its residents. Specifically, consider for each community area of Chicago the number of families with incomes below $1,000, from $1,000–1,999, from $2,000–2,999, and so forth. For the city as a whole in 1960, 44 per cent of all families with an income below $1,000 were non-white, as were 44 per cent of families with incomes from $1,000–1,999, and 40 per cent of families with incomes from $2,000–2,999. For each community area, we can apply these city-wide percentages to the observed income distribution to obtain the number of non-white families expected if income alone determined the residential locations of whites and non-whites.

By the method of indirect standardization just outlined, we obtain an expected number of non-white and white families for each of the seventy-five community areas. We can then compute an index of residential segregation between expected numbers of non-white and white families. This index can be regarded as the amount of racial residential segregation attributable to patterns of residential differentiation of

TABLE 3

Selected Socioeconomic Characteristics (Unstandardized)
of Puerto Ricans and Non-Whites, Chicago, 1960

Characteristic	Non-White	Puerto Rican
Residential segregation vs. whites	83	67
Per cent high school graduates, total	29	11
Median family income	$4,742	$4,161
Per cent families earning <$3,000	28	27
Per cent families earning >$10,000	9	4
Per cent home-owners	16	6
Per cent substandard dwellings	26	33
Per cent 1.01 or more persons per room	34	52
Per cent housing units built since 1940	12	6
Median gross rent	$88	$79
Median number of rooms	3.9	3.7
Median number of persons	3.0	4.0

Source: Data are from the 1960 Census Tract Bulletin for Chicago.

income groups. For 1950, the index of residential segregation between the numbers of whites and non-whites expected on the basis of income was 11, as compared with the actual segregation index of 79. As a rough measure, then, we can attribute 11/79, or 14 per cent, of the observed racial residential segregation in Chicago in 1950 to income differentials between whites and non-whites. For 1960, the corresponding values are 10 for the expected index, 83 for the observed index, and 12 per cent for the racial segregation attributable to income differentials.

In a recent study of the relationships between housing consumption and income, Reid has demonstrated many pitfalls in the uncritical use of income distributions in the analysis of housing patterns.[12] We have therefore repeated the above analyses, using distributions by major occupational groups and distributions by educational attainment. For 1960, the index of residential segregation computed from the numbers of whites and non-whites expected on the basis of patterns of occupational differentiation is 9, and that expected on the basis of patterns of educational differentiation is 3. The results using income distributions are thus supported by the results from other measures of socioeconomic status, and the conclusion seems clear that patterns of socioeconomic differentiation of residential areas can account for only a small proportion of observed racial residential segregation.

Reid demonstrated that differences between whites and non-whites in observed patterns of housing consumption are largely attributable to income differentials between whites and non-whites. Our analysis suggests that residential segregation cannot be attributed to these differentials. Apparently the economic structure of the housing market for whites is similar to that for non-whites, even though non-whites are excluded from a large share of the housing supply for which their economic circumstances would allow them to compete.

*   *   *

Our definition of assimilation as involving socioeconomic advancement and residential dispersion is simple, and greater differences between groups would appear were a more complex definition adopted. Restriction of portions of the analysis to the city of Chicago had little effect on the measures for non-whites, but probably led to an understatement of the degree of assimilation of the immigrant stocks insofar as higher-status members of these groups have moved to the suburbs. The segregation indexes probably overstate somewhat the residential isolation of small groups, such as particular immigrant stocks, as compared with large groups such as total native whites of native parents. Taking account of any of these limitations in our data would tend to increase the differences between Negroes and immigrant groups. . . .

In view of the fundamental impact of residential segregation on extralegal segregation of schools, hospitals, parks, stores, and numerous other facilities, the failure of residential dispersion to occur strikes us as an especially serious social problem. Socioeconomic advance and residential dispersion occurred simultaneously for the various immigrant groups. It is apparent that the continued residential segregation of the Negro population is an impediment to the continued "assimilation" of Negroes into full and equal participation in the economy and the society at large.

NOTES

1. For a more detailed discussion of these patterns, using data for 1930 and 1950, see Otis Dudley Duncan and Stanley Lieberson, "Ethnic Segregation and Assimilation," *American Journal of Sociology,* LXIV (January, 1959), 364–74.
2. Stanley Lieberson, *Ethnic Patterns in American Cities* (New York: Free Press of Glencoe, 1963).
3. For a discussion of class residential segregation in Chicago see Otis Dudley Duncan and Beverly Duncan, "Residential Distribution and Occupational Stratification," *American Journal of Sociology,* LX (March, 1955), 493–503.
4. Lieberson, *op. cit.,* pp. 120–32.
5. Karl E. Taeuber, "Negro Residential Segregation, 1940–1960: Changing Trends in the Large Cities of the United States" (paper read at the Annual Meetings of the American Sociological Association, 1962).

6. David A. Wallace, "Residential Concentration of Negroes in Chicago" (unpublished Ph.D. dissertation, Harvard University, 1953).
7. Taeuber, *op. cit.*
8. Philip M. Hauser, "The Challenge of Metropolitan Growth," *Urban Land,* XVII (December, 1958), 5.
9. Although the maximum value of the residential segregation index is less than 100 for ethnic groups of small size, this is not sufficient to vitiate the Negro-Japanese comparison.
10. Harry H. L. Kitano, "Housing of Japanese-Americans in the San Francisco Bay Area," in Nathan Glazer and Davis McEntire (eds.), *Studies in Housing and Minority Groups* (Berkeley: University of California Press, 1960), p. 184.
11. A general discussion of this problem can be found in the section on explanation of areal variation in Otis Dudley Duncan, Ray P. Cuzzort, and Beverly Duncan, *Statistical Geography* (Glencoe, Ill.: Free Press, 1961).
12. Margaret G. Reid, *Housing and Income* (Chicago: University of Chicago Press, 1962).

PRICE DISCRIMINATION AGAINST NEGROES IN THE RENTAL HOUSING MARKET

Chester Rapkin

Considerable controversy surrounds the question of whether housing market discrimination and segregation force Negroes to pay more than whites for housing of comparable size and quality. Professor Rapkin examines this question, using sample data from the 1960 census, and concludes that Negroes do obtain less housing for their money than whites because of discrimination. Moreover, he concludes that this price discrimination intensifies as the rent level increases. Chester Rapkin is a Professor of Urban Planning and Director of the Institute of Urban Environment at Columbia University.

In the mid-1960's, residential segregation and its accompanying economic inequities remains as one of the last major barriers to the cultural integration of Negroes in American life. . . . Because it has created a type of price discrimination inimical to the principles of a free market, it has also had a direct effect on the quality of housing

Author's Acknowledgements: I wish to express my appreciation to Dr. Grace Milgram, for her invaluable assistance during the entire course of this study; and to Mr. Gene Milgram. Certain original data used in this paper were derived from a punch card file furnished under a joint project sponsored by the U.S. Bureau of Census and the Population Council and containing selected 1960 census information having a 0.1 per cent sample of the population of the United States. Neither the Census Bureau nor the Population Council assumes any responsibility for the validity of any of the figures or the interpretations of the figures published herein.

From "Price Discrimination Against Negroes in the Rental Housing Market," by Chester Rapkin. Excerpted and reprinted from *Essays in Urban Land Economics* (Los Angeles: Real Estate Research Program, University of California, 1966) by permission of Housing, Real Estate & Urban Land Studies Program, University of California, Los Angeles, and Chester Rapkin.

and on our ability to achieve a major national goal of a sound and attractive dwelling for every American family.

It should not come as news that Negroes as a group occupy inferior housing, but the prevalence of such inequality may be astonishing to some. The Census of 1960 showed that 44 per cent of Negro households then lived in substandard quarters (i.e., in housing units that were in need of substantial repair or that lacked necessary plumbing facilities). Nevertheless this disturbing situation represented an improvement over previous years, for as recently as a decade earlier 72 per cent of Negro households were in substandard units. Thus a comparison of the two decades does show that the average quality of American housing is moving upward and that the Negro people are sharing in the benefits. Despite its marked improvement, however, the Negro housing situation is far worse than that of white households, for whom the incidence of substandard occupancy was 13 per cent in 1960, and 32 per cent in 1950.

Many explanations can be offered for the inferior housing status of the Negro people. The most obvious is their limited purchasing power when compared with the rest of the nation; the median Negro income is approximately 55 per cent of that of the white. And since the income gap is so great, it seems reasonable to assume that differences in purchasing power alone can account for the greater incidence of substandard units. But although there is no doubt that the quality of housing correlates negatively with income, the incidence of substandard units is higher in every income category, for owners as well as for renter Negro families.

It has been further suggested that the poor condition of housing occupied by Negroes is due to the fact that, compared with that of whites, housing occupies an inferior position in the scale of Negro consumer preference. If this were generally true, then the housing expenditures in each income class would be less for Negroes than for whites. And this is so in many housing market areas. The trouble with this thesis, however, is that in many other areas the reverse is also true. The problem, then, is to explain the departure, regardless of its direction, assuming of course that it is not random; for, given a free market, there is no prior reason why any variance should occur. If there were a tendency to spend less on housing, it would imply a greater social preference, or a physical need for more of other commodities, or that the tendency to save is the greater; all three assumptions, however, are difficult to establish.

The only thesis that explains these statistical anomalies is the flat statement that the poorer condition of Negro housing arises from discriminatory treatment in the housing market, so that the purchasing power of the dollar spent by nonwhites is less than that of the dollar spent by whites. This view has been widely held by housing econo-

mists, as well as by students of race relations. Possibly the only dis-
senting opinion has come from Margaret Reid,[1] who holds that if
permanent income is considered, income for income Negroes pay the
same rent and receive the same space and quality as whites. Any
exception results from their recent immigration into large cities, she
maintains, rather than from operation of a discriminatory or segregated
market. Their recent urbanization, she believes, has produced dis-
advantages in knowledge and the ability to acquire housing from the
sitting population. Not only is Dr. Reid's major conclusion at variance
with the body of opinion and evidence, but data presented later in
this paper cast doubt on the exception to her general statement.

If price discrimination is assumed to exist, then the differences, posi-
tive or negative, between the rent-income ratio of Negroes and whites
can be explained by dividing Negro households into two groups. Where
the Negro families seek the same housing standards as whites in
comparable income brackets, they are compelled to pay more to
obtain accommodations of the quality available to whites at lower
rentals, which of course will lead to higher rent-income ratios. This
economic consumption phenomenon is all the more pronounced be-
cause Negroes of lower occupation and income status than whites in
comparable groups tend to adopt middle-class patterns of life. It may
therefore be suggested that the greater the upward social mobility of
the Negro, the higher his rent-income ratio is likely to be, compared
with the ratios of whites in similar income categories.

Where there is relatively little social mobility, or where Negroes lack
middle-class aspirations, there will be a tendency for their rent-income
ratios to be lower than those of whites in similar income categories.
The Negro in this group acts as an economic man attempting to obtain
a dollar's worth of goods for every dollar expended. His expenditures
on food, consumer durables, automobiles, clothing, and other com-
modities are in the general American market, whereas he suffers from
price discrimination in the housing market, where he gets less than a
dollar's worth of goods for a dollar. Under these circumstances, hous-
ing cannot compete successfully for the Negro consumer's dollar, and
he will therefore be inclined to spend less of his income on housing
than will whites in similar income groups.

But despite the many variations that are found in rent expenditure
patterns, the overall average across the metropolitan United States
shows that in every rent class the median rent-income ratio of Negro
renters is higher than that of whites, and regardless of income Negroes
show a higher proportion of substandard units than do whites (Table 1).

*   *   *

Another possible explanation for this apparent inequity lies not in
discriminatory treatment, but in the amount of space used. Since

TABLE 1 *

Characteristics of Renter-Occupied Housing Units, Total and Nonwhite,
Inside SMSA's for the United States: 1960

Monthly Gross Rent	Median Rent-Income Ratio		Per Cent Substandard		Median Number of Rooms		Per Cent More Than One Person/Room	
	Total	Non-white	Total	Non-white	Total	Non-white	Total	Non-white
Total	24.9	26.1	20.7	41.2	3.8	3.2	14.0	28.5
Less than $30	19.8	22.3	50.3	62.1	2.4	2.2	17.3	25.8
$ 30–$ 39	20.8	24.2	42.9	56.3	2.7	2.4	16.5	28.5
$ 40–$ 49	19.6	24.3	36.8	50.9	3.1	2.6	17.3	29.2
$ 50–$ 59	19.0	23.9	29.3	44.5	3.4	3.0	17.0	30.0
$ 60–$ 69	19.2	24.8	23.2	39.1	3.6	3.2	16.5	29.9
$ 70–$ 79	19.8	24.8	17.8	33.9	3.8	3.4	14.5	28.3
$ 80–$ 99	20.4	26.2	12.9	30.6	4.1	3.7	12.7	27.9
$100–$119	21.8	28.1	8.6	27.4	4.3	4.1	11.2	27.9
$120 and over	22.1	29.4	4.5	23.9	4.6	4.7	7.8	25.7

* Source: U.S. Bureau of the Census, U.S. Census of Housing: 1960, Vol. II, Metropolitan Housing. Part 1, United States and Division.

Negro households are on the average larger than white, it is possible that they prefer more space to better quality. There are no three-way tabulations of housing units by number of rooms, condition, and rent available in the standard published material of the Census of Housing. The published data of the median number of rooms by rent for United States metropolitan areas in 1960 show that Negroes, on the whole, obtain smaller units than whites. This would lend credence to the belief that some Negroes, at least, receive worse housing and less space for their money than whites; but the questions of whether such discrimination is widespread or limited to certain rent classes and the degree to which discrimination operates have remained open.

*   *   *

The availability of the one-in-a-thousand sample from the 1960 Census has made possible a further examination of the questions of the extent and location of differences in the quality of housing of the same room count occupied by Negroes and whites at the same rent levels, as well as consideration of the degree to which recent migration to metropolitan areas might explain the existing variations in quality.[2]

Because the emphasis in this study lay not so much in the differences in housing, per se, as in whether the housing market operated in a discriminatory fashion, an effort was made to examine housing quality in comparable submarkets.

*   *   *

The data presented by the Census could be distributed only by the four major regions of the country, and within each region only by size of metropolitan area. Although older suburbs with housing in poor condition exist, for the most part there are both environmental and quality differences between housing in central cities and in other sections of the metropolitan area. Consequently housing conditions have been examined only for the central cities of metropolitan areas, separately for those in areas above and below 500,000 population, within each of the four regions. To eliminate influences which might tend to mask major differences in treatment, the study was limited to an examination of the condition of the housing of Negroes, rather than of all nonwhites, and of whites without Spanish surnames, rather than all whites. Study was further restricted to households paying monetary rent; those living in a unit without payment of cash rent, and owners whose annual housing expenditures cannot be learned from the housing census, were both excluded. Renters were divided into nine classes: those paying under $50 a month gross rent, those paying rents from $50 to $79, and those paying $80 and over; and within each rent class those living in one and two rooms, three to five rooms, and six or more rooms were included in the study.

In each region, and for each metropolitan size class separately within a region, within each of the nine classes, a comparison was made between the proportions of Negro and white households living in substandard units and similarly, between the proportions living in units of "low quality." Low quality was defined to include, in addition to substandard units, those classified as deteriorating yet having all plumbing facilities and those lacking central heat or private cooking facilities. A chi-square test was performed to determine the statistical significance in each cell of the differences in the proportion of substandard and of low quality units occupied by whites and Negroes.

*   *   *

When the proportion of substandard units is examined, certain patterns emerge which hold with minor variations throughout the country, and in both metropolitan area size classes. Separate tables were prepared for each region of the country. The three regions outside of the South show much the same pattern. The lower housing quality obtained by Negroes when renting dwellings is pervasive; it persists in virtually all rent classes and all size units, except one- and two-room units renting for less than $50, in center cities of larger metropolitan areas outside of the South (Table 2). Despite this major exception, it is more than evident that Negroes spending the same rent as whites to rent the same number of rooms obtain a substantially greater proportion of substandard units.

TABLE 2

Percentage of Substandard Units by Rent Class and Number of Rooms, for Center Cities of Metropolitan Areas with Less and More than 500,000 Population, by Race: South, U.S. other than South, and U.S., 1960

Rent Class	Number of Rooms					
	1–2		3–5		6 and over	
	White	Negro	White	Negro	White	Negro
I. Center Cities in Metropolitan Areas with 500,000 or More						
A. Total U.S.						
Less than $50	72.0	71.4	20.7	33.0	11.5	14.3
$50–$79	23.6	57.8	7.9	18.6	4.9	25.0
$80 and over	8.7	41.7	1.4	9.4	2.0	15.5
B. South						
Less than $50	63.8	77.1	18.3	38.6	33.3	50.0
$50–$79	16.2	41.2	7.3	22.3	8.3	41.2
$80 and over	4.8	25.0	.5	—	5.3	17.4
C. U.S. Other than South						
Less than $50	73.1	69.0	21.0	27.8	8.7	—
$50–$79	24.9	60.4	8.0	16.9	4.6	17.9
$80 and over	9.1	43.8	1.6	10.9	1.7	14.9
II. Center Cities in Metropolitan Areas with Less than 500,000						
A. Total U.S.						
Less than $50	70.6	97.4	26.5	53.8	20.0	14.3
$50–$79	27.5	46.7	10.5	43.1	12.8	55.6
$80 and over	16.7	—	.7	4.3	2.2	44.4
B. South						
Less than $50	55.8	100.0	19.7	55.9	25.0	16.7
$50–$79	17.6	66.7	6.5	48.1	16.7	83.3
$80 and over	12.5	—	—	—	2.4	33.3
C. U.S. Other than South						
Less than $50	77.4	83.3	30.4	33.3	16.7	—
$50–$79	32.4	33.3	12.6	28.0	11.7	—
$80 and over	18.8	—	1.1	6.3	2.1	50.0

The exception is in itself interesting, exemplifying two other strands of the pattern. Throughout the country, regardless of the race of the occupant, there is a sharp distinction between the quality of one and two-room units and units with a higher room count. This is particularly true of the low-rent small units, over 70 per cent of which in center cities of all metropolitan areas are substandard. In fact, in the smaller metropolitan areas all one- and two-room units occupied by Negroes in the South, and over 80 per cent of those in the rest of the country, are substandard. In more expensive units, the incidence of substandard units is not so great, but even in the middle range, a quarter of those occupied by whites and over half of those occupied by Negroes are substandard, as are one-tenth of white-occupied and two-fifths of the Negro-occupied small units renting for $80 or more a month.

Since the proportion of substandard units among the larger apartments is considerably lower, there arises the question of why anyone would rent a small substandard unit when apparently he could obtain a larger standard accomodation for the same rental. In part, the answer may lie in the complete unavailability of larger units. The more likely explanation, however, is the fact that small units frequently offer quite different services, providing not only space but furniture, weekly rather than monthly rent payments, and the possibility of not being bound by a lease. The price for these additional services may be met not only by cash rent but also by low quality. Finding the explanation, however, lies beyond the scope of this study.

The group of one- and two-room units renting for less than $50 a month shows the impact not only of the difference in the small unit market, but also of the low rent. Not surprisingly, the incidence of substandard quality in central cities across the nation is greatest in units renting for less than $50, averaging 44 per cent for white-occupied units and 53 per cent for Negro-occupied; in the $50 to $79 rental class, the figures drop to 11 and 29 per cent; and for rentals of $80 and over the drop is to 2 and 14 per cent.

While the variation displayed between rental classes is to be expected, the lack of a consistent pattern within rental classes is surprising. It has been assumed generally that more rooms could be obtained at the same rental only at the cost of poorer condition; and the question that was to be examined, of course, was whether Negroes substituted space for quality to a different degree than did whites. Thus it might be expected that within any rental class the proportion of substandard units would be higher, the greater the number of rooms rented. We have already seen that one- and two-room units do in fact have the highest proportion of substandard units, and we have assumed that they therefore represent a distinct submarket offering services different from those of the rest of the rental housing stock. But it is only in the South that the expected increase between proportion substandard in three-to-five and six-room units occurs.

*　　*　　*

Another explanation for quality differences which was tested was the possibility that recent inmigrants to the metropolitan area had greater difficulty in obtaining standard units than did the sitting population. The condition of housing occupied by those of the same race who had moved to the metropolitan area from a noncontiguous state within the preceding five years was examined separately from housing occupied by all others. The results are shown in Table 3, for the central cities of the entire United States. As can be seen, there is no

TABLE 3

Percentage of Substandard Units, by Rent Class and Number of Rooms for Sitting Population and Inmigrants of Central Cities of Metropolitan Areas, by Race: United States, 1960

| Rent Class | Number of Rooms | | | | | |
| | 1 and 2 | | 3–5 | | 6 and over | |
	Sitting Population	Inmigrants*	Sitting Population	Inmigrants*	Sitting Population	Inmigrants*
	A.	White				
Less than $50	71.4	76.2	21.3	30.0	14.8	11.1
$50–$79	24.6	18.5	9.1	3.4	8.6	2.8
$80 and over	9.0	20.0	1.3	1.9	2.0	3.1
	B.	Negro				
Less than $50	78.7	62.5	39.7	73.7	14.3	—
$50–$79	57.1	33.3	22.5	29.2	30.6	—
$80 and over	38.2	66.7	8.9	12.5	19.2	—

* Inmigrants were defined as all households headed by persons whose place of residence in 1955 had been in any noncontiguous state. All others, including households headed by persons whose place of residence was in the same metropolitan areas, in the same state, or in a contiguous state, were included in the sitting population.

regular difference between the proportion of substandard dwellings occupied by those resident for five years or more, and those of less than five years; nor are the differences in the cells of either Negroes or whites statistically significant. Length of residence, then, would not seem to have any systematic effect upon the quality of housing obtained.

From a social viewpoint, possibly the most important observation which can be made from these tables is not the fact that discriminatory treatment exists, a confirmation of a view long held by housing economists, but rather that the degree of discrimination appears to increase markedly as Negroes approach middle class status. The data show that in general the incidence of substandard housing decreases as rent paid increases, for both whites and Negroes, but the decrease is considerably greater for whites than for Negroes. If all cities are examined, the proportion of substandard among the smallest units was almost equal in the lowest rent class, approximately twice as great for Negro-occupied units renting for $50 to $79, and over four times as great in those renting for over $80. In the three-to-five-room units, the ratio of the proportions of substandard units increased from under twice as much to over seven times as great. In the largest units, the proportion decreased among whites, but actually increased for Negro-occupied units, as rent rose from less than $50 to $50–$79; then it decreased in the highest rent category, but not quite to the level of the group under $50. In all units in central cities of the country, taken as a whole, the proportion of substandard in Negro units was approximately one-fifth greater than in white-occupied units, for those renting under $50, and six times greater for those renting for over $80.

Increased price discrimination in the higher rent brackets may be accounted for by the fact that middle class Negroes seeking accommodations commensurate with their income and attainments find it either difficult or against their taste to select an accommodation in a segregated area; they are therefore compelled (or impelled) to seek an apartment in an area that is largely or entirely occupied by white families. Although race restrictions are disappearing in some cities in the North, it is usually extremely difficult for a Negro family to obtain quarters under these circumstances, because the mechanisms of exclusion are powerful and difficult to combat. Moreover, they are used with great frequency because the landlord fears his white tenants will resent a new neighbor of a different color. Resistance to Negro occupancy is likely to be less marked if an apartment has been vacant a long time and if the prospect of renting it to a white family in the near future is slim. Apartments in this category are usually poor value for the money, which means that their rent is in excess of the market level for apartments of similar size, quality, and location.

The intensification of price discrimination in the higher rent ranges has undoubtedly fortified the great impulse to home ownership among the middle-class Negroes. The enhancement of status which accompanies home ownership would undoubtedly have motivated many middle-class Negroes, even if their treatment in the rental market had been the same as for whites. Price discrimination makes the purchase of a home virtually the only way in which the middle-class Negro family can obtain a superior accommodation in a better neighborhood. In the cities of the North, home ownership rose between 75 to 150 per cent during the decade of the 1950's; in the West, the increase was from 125 to 175 per cent; and in the South, from 50 to 100 per cent.[3]

*   *   *

As far as the upwardly mobile Negro is concerned, the results of this study understate the discrimination practiced against him and the difficulties placed in his way by the housing market. Even within center cities, neighborhoods differ in the community facilities available to them and the undesirable uses which impinge upon the residential structures. Though low-rent housing occupied by whites may be in as unpleasant a location as that available to Negroes, neighborhoods in which more expensive housing restricted to whites is located are generally superior to those in which equally expensive housing is available to Negroes. And insofar as Negroes able to afford more expensive housing share the customary American middle-class view that the suburban environment is preferable to that in the center city, even those Negroes who succeed in finding housing of standard quality are obtaining less desirable units than those of whites who move to suburbia or who voluntarily rent in the city because they prefer it. Thus, the Negro who achieves middle-class status is rewarded in the housing market by an increasing burden of price and locational discrimination.

NOTES

1. Margaret Reid, *Housing and Home* (Chicago: University of Chicago Press, 1962), p. 389.
2. For details on the composition of the sample see: U.S. Census of Population and Housing: 1960, *1/1000 and 1/10,000, Two National Samples of the Population of the United States, Description and Technical Documentations.*
3. For a discussion of the housing problems of the middle-class Negro see Chester Rapkin, "More Housing For Negroes," *The Mortgage Banker,* February 1964.

THE GHETTO MAKERS

Jack Rothman

Real estate agents and financial institutions play a critical role in the housing market. Jack Rothman, a social psychologist and social worker, identifies two kinds of real estate brokers, the "block busters" and the "lily-whiters," and describes their roles and those of banks and mortgage lenders in maintaining and intensifying residential segregation.

Meet a group of ugly Americans you probably don't know—the "Ghetto Makers." They are found primarily in the real-estate and money-lending worlds and their stock in trade is racism for a profit. These are the men who control and manipulate the housing market in integrated areas of our cities. They specialize in panic salesmanship —the rumor, the racial argument, the prejudicial insinuation. They engage in a variety of pernicious financial practices, both legal and extra-legal, taking the Negro home-buyer for a ride in the process. Through their pressure-cooker tactics, whole neighborhoods are induced to change from white to colored—and segregated—in short order, and at great cost in human terms.

Racially changing neighborhoods have in recent years reached widespread and troubling proportions. Almost every city-dweller can call to mind some neighborhood that was transformed almost overnight from a solidly white to a solidly Negro district. . . .

One of the chief causes of rapid neighborhood change (and consequently of residential segregation) is the presence of prejudice in so many of our white citizens. No sooner does the first Negro family move into a white area than large numbers of whites move out. But this prejudice constitutes only the most obvious starting point in attempting to understand the dynamics of the change pattern. What is

From "The Ghetto Makers" by Jack Rothman, *The Nation*, 193, No. 10 (October 7, 1961), 222–25. Excerpted and reprinted by permission of *The Nation*.

less known is that in addition to this "spontaneous" process, there are purposeful, efficiently organized "unspontaneous" influences at work— the Ghetto Makers, who consciously trigger off these personal pre-dispositions and channel them into large-scale movements. These Ghetto Makers play at least as large a part in fostering segregation as do public attitudes and their role needs to be laid bare and under-stood if we are ever to make headway in coping with the problem.

Standing at their head are a core of unethical or prejudiced real-estate brokers. In the course of directing an experimental citizens' project aimed at stabilizing a racially changing neighborhood, I had a chance to observe a representative group of these brokers at first hand. The project, sponsored by the community planning division of the New York City Youth Board, was centered in the middle-class residen-tial community of Springfield Gardens in the Borough of Queens.

The brokers I observed seemed to fall into two categories which may be described as the "block-busters" and the "lily-whiters." The block-busters are the more deliberately destructive. Once a Negro somehow manages to move into a white neighborhood, these brokers make their entrance and work over the area. Through house-to-house canvassing, relentless telephone solicitation, use of the mails and by various other means, they create an atmosphere of panic in the neighborhood and high-pressure the white residents into selling. They open up one block at a time, saturating block A with Negroes and then going on to block B. "Do you want your kids to play with colored kids?" goes their sales talk. "Do you want to be the last white family left on the block? Do you want to lose a fortune on your house?" Characteristically, they approach a home owner with a cash offer and the (often fallacious) news that Mrs. Jones down the street is selling to a Negro family. Emphasis is placed on the urgency of selling immediately, before the value of the house nose-dives. Occasionally "decoys," such as a Negro woman wheeling a baby carriage, are paraded up and down the street to set the proper psychological climate.

For the realty salesman, the wholesale turnover of an entire area is a happy and enormously profitable prospect. By panicking home own-ers, the broker can pocket an even greater return by entering the market he is manipulating, buying low and selling high. Negro brokers as well as whites avail themselves of the block-busting tech-nique; actually, the Negro brokers are even more insidious, since they are so heavily relied on by their Negro clients.

The block-busting real-estate men show homes in integrated districts such as Springfield Gardens only to prospective Negro buyers; I have known them deliberately to turn down prospective white buyers. For them the steady and total segregation of the neighborhood is a desir-able goal.

Meanwhile the other real-estate brokers, the lily-whiters, are operating in white areas adjacent to the changing community. Their clientele is usually entirely white. I saw them operating in Laurelton, adjacent to Springfield Gardens. If these Laurelton brokers had made an effort to show homes in contiguous integrated areas to their clients (as indeed had been their custom prior to integration), there would have been a greater possibility of counterbalancing the influence of the blockbusters and maintaining a racially mixed community. However, we found that these lily-white brokers consistently failed to show homes in these areas to white clients, and turned down listings from Springfield Gardens which were offered to them. Just a few Negro families in an area marked it off-limits to these brokers for showing homes to white buyers. Their reasons for taking this position range from their own conscious or unconscious prejudices ("What decent person would want to live in that area anyway?") to realistic economic considerations (it takes less time and effort to place the average white buyer in a white community than in an integrated one; and time is money).

Because of the extensive activity in the integrated areas of the blockbusters and the abandonment of the areas by the lily-whiters, each time a house is placed on the market it is sold to a Negro family. This results usually in a gradual and unswerving rise in the percentage of Negro residents in a given community.

Banks and lending institutions also play their unsavory part in this operation. They not only make it difficult for non-whites to obtain a mortgage when they attempt to buy in a white area; they also discriminate against whites who want to buy in a changing neighborhood. The banks take the view that a white individual who moves into a mixed area will soon find himself part of a small minority and will consequently move out within a short period of time, thus diminishing the duration of the loan. In one case, our committee had to contact a dozen banks before the enlightened Bowery Savings in downtown Manhattan agreed to make a loan to a financially solid white family.

Advertising in the Negro press is still another facet of Ghetto Making. Extensive and dramatic advertising directed at the Negro community is placed by brokers who specialize in changing communities. Brokers located in the major districts of Negro settlements like Harlem, and Bedford-Stuyvesant in Brooklyn, play up these areas with gigantic signs, flyleafs, etc. Since often such locations are the only sources of decent residential property for Negroes, this activity is entirely understandable. It tends, however, to make more difficult the process of orderly neighborhood change, and to foster segregation.

In advertisements in the Negro press (placed by both white and Negro brokers), one detects a pattern of unethical, even fraudulent, practices. Homes are advertised at unrealistically low prices to attract naive purchasers. Example of a typical ad:

Magnificent home, $29.00 a month pays all. Detached 2-family, plus a rentable 3-room basement apartment. Really living rent free. Situated in a tremendous garden plot. Modern kitchen, Cadillac-size garage, automatic heat, three bedrooms and extras galore. $890.00 down.

When a Negro teacher acquaintance of mine responded to such an ad, he was first told the property was located in an isolated swamp area near Idlewild International Airport and that he wouldn't really be interested in it. Later the broker admitted that the ad was a "come on." The objective is to entice the prospective buyer into the office by any suitable means at hand. Then an attempt is made to sell him a more expensive home.

The uninformed buyer is encouraged to overcrowd the house by using the attic and basement to take in roomers, boarders, foster children, etc., often in direct violation of existing housing ordinances. . . . Most brokers who speak loftily of "neighborhood homogeneity" when it comes to keeping a neighborhood white, do not at all respect the concept of a homogeneous *middle-class* neighborhood when applied to Negroes. They willingly inject lower-class and "problematic" elements into an evolving middle-class Negro or interracial community, thus thwarting the efforts of colored teachers, doctors, lawyers and businessmen to enjoy the benefits of a reasonable standard of community living for themselves and their children.

As people who cannot afford payment for homes are deliberately enticed into brokers' offices, funding companies associated with the brokers make loans through devious and highly questionable financing methods. The result is that the purchasers are led into debt over their heads and find it necessary to overcrowd their homes for extra income. Again, a middle-class area tends to break down into a segregated slum.

* * *

The intricate financial machinations of the Ghetto Makers could make up a field of study in its own right. I will describe here only techniques I personally witnessed in the project area. Similar techniques, with appropriate local adaptations, have been put into effect in communities across the country and have been amply documented. . . .

In the Queens instance, funding companies affiliated with brokers required a large number of "points" to complete the purchase of a home. Each point is 1 per cent of the mortgage (for example, $150 on a $15,000 mortgage) and consists of a kind of service charge for making the loan. Since often the Negro purchaser, drawn into the broker's office through one of the beguiling hawking methods described above, does not have enough money for the down payment, he cannot obtain a loan directly from an ordinary bank, which might require only one or two points. He is therefore at the mercy of the funding companies, which in some cases have been known to demand up to 12 per cent of the mortgage (twelve points) merely for making the loan. This is independent of any interest rates on the loan. . . .

But this is not the end of the story. We now have a Negro buyer paying a high number of points, and unable to afford even a sufficient down payment. A contract of sale is made, permitting the purchaser to occupy the house; he must, however, pay a monthly bill until he has met the down payment. There is no actual transfer of title or deed until the down payment is completely paid off—ordinarily a matter of some five to seven years. Only then do the payments on the actual mortgage begin. During these first years, the monthly payment includes not only the down-payment installment, but also interest on the down payment, interest on the old mortgage, carrying charges on the house such as taxes, insurance, water and sewage bills, etc. All this time *the purchaser has no security whatever.* Should he fail to meet a monthly payment, he may lose the house and every cent he has so far put into it.

The whole operational scheme of the Ghetto Makers makes sense only in the light of the undemocratic and socially debilitating ground rules under which our racial minorities live. While choked for space in depressed slum area, Negroes are rigorously restricted in the housing market, with almost no new housing being constructed to meet their needs. . . . It is no wonder that as a particular area of the city opens up for non-white occupancy, the Negro market will flow in that direction, all other channels being blocked. Thus, the slightly integrated community rather quickly becomes the changing community and, with a solid assist by the Ghetto Makers, eventually becomes the totally segregated Negro community.

This pattern can be reversed only when our cities achieve an open-occupancy status compatible with our democratic precepts. Under these circumstances, Negro families could disperse themselves widely into many neighborhoods in accordance with their economic resources.

Such an end can be achieved only by eliminating racial restrictions on home ownership and, simultaneously, striking hard at the Ghetto Makers, the shysters and manipulators of the housing market. No legislation currently on the books is geared toward specific control of the Ghetto Makers' practices I have described. There are Fair Housing Practices bills in some cities (notably New York and Pittsburgh) and states (notably Colorado, Connecticut, Massachusetts and more recently New York) which deal with discrimination in housing.

But none has a Fair Selling Practices clause which effectively regulates the block-busters until a state of open occupancy is achieved.

Likewise, no existing law can deal adequately with some of the elaborate, racist financing and advertising techniques devised by the Ghetto Makers.

The Ghetto Makers exert power in present-day America. They decide whom you may live next to and who may live next to you. For this service they extract a huge profit. The power of these men may be broken by legal means coupled with the weight of an enlightened public opinion.

PART IV

Attitudes: White and Black

WHITE ATTITUDES TOWARD THE NEGRO

Paul B. Sheatsley

Prejudice by whites against Negroes obviously bears a large part of the responsibility for the existence and maintenance of discriminatory practices. Current white attitudes toward discrimination and integration will be crucial in determining the success of programs designed to reduce discrimination and provide greater opportunities for Negroes. Paul B. Sheatsley uses several surveys of white attitudes conducted between 1942 and 1967 to assess the attitudes of different groups and the secular changes in their attitudes toward discrimination, integration, and other aspects of Negro-white relations. Mr. Sheatsley is Director of the Survey Research Service of the National Opinion Research Center at the University of Chicago.

. . . Proper interpretation of survey data requires some baseline or norm against which a particular finding can be evaluated. While it is of interest to know, for instance, that "eight in ten white Americans said they would not move" if a Negro family moved next door, or that 41 per cent feel that the pace of civil rights progress is too fast,[1] the numbers have little meaning unless we can anchor them somehow. One means of anchoring is to compare findings over the course of time. The figures take on added significance if we can determine whether they are increasing or decreasing in response to events. A second means is to compare subgroup differences (for example, North vs. South, the well-educated vs. those with little formal education)

From "White Attitudes Toward the Negro" by Paul B. Sheatsley, *Daedalus, The Negro American-2*, 95, No. 1 (Winter, 1966), 217–38. Excerpted and reprinted by permission of *Daedalus*, Journal of the American Academy of Arts and Sciences, Boston, Mass., and Paul B. Sheatsley.

against the national norm. We propose to examine past and current survey findings with a view to clarifying and interpreting their meaning. In the course of this examination we shall rely mainly, though not exclusively, on data gathered by the National Opinion Research Center of the University of Chicago.

TWENTY-YEAR TRENDS ON SCHOOL INTEGRATION [2]

Chart I shows for each of three years—1942, 1956, and 1963—the proportion of American whites who expressed approval of integra-

CHART I

Per Cent Who Say White Students and Negro Students Should Go to the Same Schools

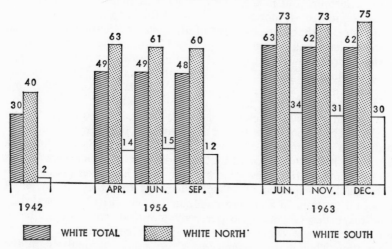

(This is an adaptation of a chart which appeared in an article by H. H. Hyman and P. B. Sheatsley, "Attitudes Toward Desegregation," *Scientific American*, Vol. 211, July 1964. Copyright © 1964 by *Scientific American*, Inc. All rights reserved.)

tion when asked the question, "Do you think white students and Negro students should go to the same schools or to separate schools?" [3] The most striking message of the chart is the revolutionary change in white attitudes, both North and South,[4] which has taken place on this explosive issue in less than a generation. In 1942, not one American white in three approved of integrated schools. Even in the North, majority sentiment was strongly opposed, while in the South only two whites in one hundred could be found to support the proposition. By 1956, two years after the historic Supreme Court decision which abolished the "separate but equal" doctrine, white attitudes had shifted markedly. Nationwide, support for integration was now characteristic of about half the white population, while in the North it had clearly become the majority view. In the South, where only one white person in fifty had favored integration fourteen years earlier, the proportion by 1956 had risen to approximately one in seven.

The continuation of the trend from 1956 to 1963 is especially noteworthy, since the years between were marked by agitation and occasional violence which might easily have led one to suspect a reversal of attitudes and a white revulsion against integration. . . . But repetition of the same question to three different national samples in 1963 showed that this massive trend was still intact. By that year, almost two-thirds of all American whites expressed approval of integrated schools; among white persons in the North, the proportion was close to three in four. And in the South, which was then bearing the brunt of the Negro protest movement, sentiment for integration had climbed even faster, so that almost a third of all white Southerners agreed that white students and Negro students should attend the same schools.

The figures shown on the chart for the South represent, of course, a geographical composite of Deep South states like Mississippi and Alabama, border states such as West Virginia and Kentucky, and southwestern states such as Arkansas and Oklahoma. We shall indicate certain regional differences later. It is possible, however, to sort the Southern respondents to the 1963 surveys into three groups, according to the amount of school integration in their communities. When this is done, it is found that a solid majority of Southern whites (58 per cent), in those few places where there had been (as of 1963) considerable integration of schools, declared that they approved of school integration. In Southern communities which had accepted only some token desegregation, 38 per cent approved; while in the hard-core segregationist communities, only 28 per cent were in favor of integration. Though the sample sizes are small, particularly in the desegregated areas, the correlation is clear: Where integration exists in the South, more whites support it.[5]

It is dangerous to try to unravel cause and effect from mere statistical correlation, yet a close analysis of the data indicates that official action to desegregate Southern schools did not wait for majority opinion to demand it, but rather preceded a change in community attitudes. In the 1956 surveys, only 31 per cent of Southern whites in those few areas which had begun at least token desegregation expressed approval of integrated schools. Clearly there was no public demand for integration in those areas then. Furthermore, by 1963 the integrated areas included not only those communities which had pioneered in integration in 1956, but also many additional communities where anti-integration sentiment had in 1956 been even stronger. Yet by 1963 the majority of Southern whites in such communities had accepted the integration of their schools. It may be noted that even in the most segregationist parts of the South, approval of integration has continued to climb. In 1956, only 4 per cent of Southern whites residing in segregated school areas approved of integration, but by 1963 the proportion in communities which had not by then introduced even token integration—the essential "hard-core" areas—had nevertheless risen to 28 per cent.

TRENDS ON OTHER RACIAL ISSUES

School integration is one of the most basic and explosive of the civil rights issues, and it has provided perhaps the most apt illustration of the dramatic shift in white attitudes over the past two decades. Additional evidence from the same surveys is available, however, to show that the increasing accommodation of whites to equal rights has not been restricted to the schools, but extends to other spheres as well. Table 1 shows the trends in attitudes with respect to residential

TABLE 1

Per Cent Who Approve Residential and Public Transportation Integration in 1942, 1956, June and December, 1963

| | Surveys in. . . . | | | |
Approval of . . .	1942	1956	June 1963	Dec. 1963
Residential Integration				
National white total	35	51	61	64
Northern whites only	42	58	68	70
Southern whites only	12	38	44	51
Public Transportation Integration				
National white total	44	60	79	78
Northern whites only	57	73	89	88
Southern whites only	4	27	52	51

integration and the integration of public transportation. The three later surveys used exactly the same questions that were employed in 1942. These were: "If a Negro with the same income and education as you have moved into your block, would it make any difference to you?" [6] and "Generally speaking, do you think there should be separate sections for Negroes on streeetcars and buses?" Nationwide, in 1942 only 35 per cent of American whites would not have objected to a

Negro neighbor of their own social class; by 1963 almost two out of
three would accept such a neighbor. Nationwide, in 1942 fewer than
half of all American whites approved of integrated transportation
facilities; by 1963 almost four out of five had adopted this view. The
changes are especially dramatic among Southern whites, for in 1942
only one out of eight of them would have accepted a Negro neighbor
and but one in twenty-five the idea of sharing transportation facilities
on an integrated basis. By the end of 1963, both forms of integration
had achieved majority approval.

*   *   *

An important shift in white beliefs on one further issue helps ex-
plain the trends we have observed and underlines the solid base on
which they rest. In 1942, a national sample of whites was asked,
"In general, do you think that Negroes are as intelligent as white people
—that is, can they learn things just as well if they are given the same
education and training?" At that time only about half the Northern
whites and one Southern white in five answered "Yes." Today, four-
fifths of the white population in the North and a substantial majority
in the South (57 per cent) believe that Negroes are as intelligent as
white people. The implications of this revolutionary change in attitudes
toward Negro educability are far-reaching. It has undermined one of
the most stubborn arguments formerly offered by whites for segregated
schools and has made the case for segregation much more difficult to
defend.

SUBGROUP DIFFERENCES IN WHITE ATTITUDES TOWARD THE NEGRO

The NORC survey of December 1963 asked a national sample of
white persons a broad range of questions designed to measure their
attitudes toward Negroes and toward the civil rights movement. From
this range of questions it was possible to form a Guttman scale of
pro-integration attitudes based upon the eight items shown in Table
2.[7] The properties of a Guttman scale are such that if a person rejects
one item on the scale, the chances are at least nine in ten that he
will also reject all items below it. Thus, those who reject the top item
—equal job rights for Negroes—are highly unlikely to endorse any
of the other items on the scale and may be considered extreme segre-
gationists. At the other end of the scale, the 27 per cent who disagree
with the proposition that "Negroes shouldn't push themselves where
they're not wanted" are extremely likely to take a pro-integrationist
position on all seven of the other items.

*   *   *

TABLE 2

Guttman Scale of Pro-Integration Sentiments

Item	Per Cent Giving Pro-Integration Response (December 1963)
1. "Do you think Negroes should have as good a chance as white people to get any kind of job, or do you think white people should have the first chance at any kind of job?" ("As good a chance.")	82
2. "Generally speaking, do you think there should be separate sections for Negroes in street cars and buses?" ("No.")	77
3. "Do you think Negroes should have the right to use the same parks, restaurants, and hotels as white people?" ("Yes.")	71
4. "Do you think white students and Negro students should go to the same schools, or to separate schools?" ("Same schools.")	63
5. "How strongly would you object if a member of your family wanted to bring a Negro friend home to dinner?" ("Not at all.")	49
6. "White people have a right to keep Negroes out of their neighborhoods if they want to, and Negroes should respect that right." ("Disagree slightly" or "Disagree strongly.")	44
7. "Do you think there should be laws against marriages between Negroes and whites?" ("No.")	36
8. "Negroes shouldn't push themselves where they're not wanted." ("Disagree slightly" or "Disagree strongly.")	27

The Pro-Integration Scale provides a convenient measure of integrationist sentiment, since it is possible to assign each individual in the survey a score ranging from 0 to 8, depending upon the number of pro-integration responses he gave. From there it is a small step to compute mean (average) scores for various population groups to determine the locus of pro- and anti-civil rights attitudes. A simple calculation reveals that the mean score for all white Americans is 4.29, which indicates that the average white person accepts the first four propositions and would dislike but would not totally reject the idea of a family member bringing a Negro friend home to dinner. Table 3 shows the distribution of the mean scores among the more relevant subgroups of the white population.

Not surprisingly, the greatest differences are regional. The differences between Northern whites and Southern whites, even when such factors as age, sex, and educational level are controlled, are almost always greater than the differences between various population groups within the same region. Northern whites *in toto,* for example, have a scale score of 4.97. . . .

As of December 1963, the highest scale scores were found in the ten largest metropolitan areas, all but one of which (Washington, D.C.) are in the North (3-B). However, the date of the survey preceded the summer riots in some of these Northern cities in 1964 and the increased protests against job discrimination and *de facto* school segregation have occurred in New York, Chicago, Boston, Cleveland, and other Northern metropolises during the last year or two. Whether and to what extent these more recent events may have increased or reduced pro-integrationist attitudes in the large Northern cities is not known. It will be noted that, in both North and South, the more Negroes are integrated into the public schools, the higher the scores on the Pro-Integration Scale (3-C). There are too few Southern respondents living in areas where the schools are "considerably" integrated to justify presentation of the figure, but it is still higher than that for areas in which only a "few Negroes" attend the schools. The general finding confirms our earlier analysis of the trend data.

Turning from community variables, such as region, population size, and degree of school integration, to individual characteristics, perhaps one of the most significant findings is that shown in Part D of the table. Northerners who formerly lived in the South (and these may be either Southern migrants or Northerners who spent some time in the South) are only slightly less pro-integrationist than their neighbors who have never been exposed to Southern life. In contrast, Southerners who have previously resided in the North differ greatly from their co-regionalists who have known nothing but Southern life. The net effect of migration from one of the regions to the other seems to be a strengthening of the cause of integration. Ex-Southerners who move to the North appear generally to conform to Northern attitudes, while ex-Northerners who move to the South (and Southerners who have been temporarily exposed to Northern living) tend to reject the more extreme segregationist views of the life-long Southerner.

Men and women differ little in their scores on this Pro-Integration Scale, but age differences are more marked and are of considerable interest (3-E,F). In both North and South, the older age groups are clearly the more segregationist. The forty-five to sixty-four group has lower scores than the twenty-five to forty-four, while those sixty-five or older have the lowest scores of all. The same finding was observed in the 1956 NORC studies, and suggests that part of the long-term trend in white attitudes is due to the passing of an elderly less tolerant generation and their replacement in the population by younger adults

TABLE 3

Mean Scores on Pro-Integration Scale
(White Population, U.S.A., December 1963)

Total	North 4.97	South 2.54			North	South
A. By Region:				**F. By Age Group:**		
New England	5.03	—		Under 25	5.70	2.76
Middle Atlantic	5.47	—		25–44	5.34	2.86
East North Central	4.61	—		45–64	4.71	2.33
West North Central	4.37	—		65–up	4.07	2.10
South Atlantic	—	2.53				
East South Central	—	1.89		**G. By Religion:**		
West South Central	—	2.70				
Mountain	4.33	—		Protestant	4.75	2.38
Pacific	5.43	—		Catholic	5.18	3.41
				Jewish	6.44	a
B. By Population Size:						
				H. By Strength of Religious Belief:		
10 largest M.A.'s	5.33	a				
All other M.A.'s	4.97	2.65		Very strong	5.00	2.34
Urban counties	5.04	1.36		Strong	5.15	2.86
Rural counties	4.23	2.70		Moderate	4.87	2.53
				Not strong	4.30	2.37
C. By Number of Negroes in Public Schools:				**I. By Educational Level:**		
No Negroes	4.62	2.29		8 years or less	3.88	1.70
A few Negroes	5.01	2.80		9–12 years (H.S.)	5.01	2.71
Considerable number	5.49	a		Attended college	5.96	3.54
				J. By Family Income:		
D. By Prior Residence:						
				Under $5,000	4.36	2.20
Formerly lived in South	4.80	—		$5,000–7,499	5.24	2.75
Never lived in South	5.05	—		$7,500–9,999	5.26	2.78
				$10,000 or over	5.56	3.41
Formerly lived in North	—	3.22		**K. By Occupation:**		
Never lived in North	—	1.97		Professional	6.08	4.32
				Proprietors, managers	5.09	2.79
E. By Sex:				Clerical, sales	4.96	2.98
				Skilled	4.90	2.04
Male	4.91	2.57		Semi-skilled	4.77	1.63
Female	5.03	2.51		Unskilled	4.73	1.82
				Farm	3.86	2.87

a Insufficient cases to justify reliable answers.

who are more likely to accept racial integration. But we note a
singular inversion of the relationship between age and pro-integra-
tion sentiment among the two youngest age groups in the South. Un-
expectedly, the very youngest Southern adults (aged twenty-one to
twenty-four) have lower Pro-Integration Scale scores than the twenty-
five to forty-four year old group. The same result occurred in the June
1963 survey but not in the 1956 studies. We have suggested elsewhere[8]
that the current group of young white adults in the South have grown
up and received their schooling and formed their attitudes during the
stormy years which followed the 1954 Supreme Court decision out-
lawing segregated schools. It is they who have been most immediately
exposed to the crises and dislocations brought to the South by the
Negro protest movement. Perhaps the surprise is that these Southern
white youths today are nonetheless more pro-integrationist than are
their parents and grandparents who are over the age of forty-five.

* * *

Occupation, educational level, and family income are highly inter-
correlated and are often combined to provide a single measure of
socioeconomic status. Presented independently, as they are in Table 3
(I,J,K), they all point in the same direction, with quite remarkable
consistency. The inescapable conclusion is that the higher a person's
socioeconomic status, as measured by these three characteristics, the
higher his score on the Pro-Integration Scale. The differences by edu-
cational level are remarkably strong and have been duplicated in all
earlier NORC studies. Education is correlated with age, of course, so
that much of the differences by age which we noted earlier simply
reflects the higher educational level attained by younger adults, as
compared with their parents and grandparents. This is not to say
that education, or any other single factor, is all-important. It may be
observed that the Southern white who attended college nevertheless
has a lower scale score than the Northern white with eight years of
schooling or less. Yet, as higher proportions of the nation's youth go
on to college, as higher proportions enter white-collar and professional
rather than farm or production employment, and as (and if) family
income levels continue to rise, we may reasonably expect the long-term
trend in white attitudes toward acceptance of racial integration not
only to continue but even to accelerate.

* * *

SINCE DECEMBER 1963

We are aware that many readers will question the relevance of
public opinion poll findings from December 1963 to the situation today.
After all, the year 1964 alone saw the nomination of Barry Goldwater,

the Presidential election campaign, general elections in every state, Congressional passage of a comprehensive Civil Rights Act, Negro rioting in several Northern cities, the murder of three civil rights workers in Mississippi—to mention only some of the most striking events which might have affected the attitudes we have described. And the pace of the civil rights movement in 1965 has shown no signs of slackening. We urge such readers, however, to regain their perspective by looking again at the twenty-year trend shown in Chart 1, and especially at the absence of short-run change over the three separate surveys conducted in 1956 and 1963, when racial tensions were also high.

* * *

Opportunity to apply a more rigorous test of the hypothesis that the long-term trends are still intact finally occurred in June 1965, when NORC was able to append a few of the 1942–1963 questions to a current national survey. It was not possible to ask all of the items included in the December 1963 survey, but the measures which were obtained strongly confirmed the inexorability of the trend. The proportion of white Americans who favor school integration rose from 62 per cent to 67 per cent during this eighteen-month period, and the proportion who would not object to a Negro neighbor of the same social class rose from 64 per cent to 68 per cent. Perhaps the most striking finding was that the increases were accounted for entirely by the South. While the figures for the North held steady or showed small and insignificant fluctuations, Southern attitudes were undergoing revolutionary change. The proportion of Southern whites who favor integrated schools almost doubled within this eighteen-month period, moving from 30 per cent at the end of 1963 to 55 per cent—a clear majority—in mid-1965. The proportion of Southern whites who would not object to a Negro neighbor rose from 51 per cent to 66 per cent during this same period. Again it was found that exposure to integration fosters pro-integrationist attitudes. Of Southern whites whose children had attended school with Negroes, 74 per cent said Negroes and whites should attend the same schools; of Southern whites whose children had not attended school with Negroes, only 48 per cent held that view.

* * *

A recent (but pre-Los Angeles) Gallup Poll release confirms the remarkable change in white Southern attitudes between 1963 and 1965. In May 1963, Gallup asked a representative sample of white parents, "Would you yourself have any objection to sending your children to a school where a few of the children are colored?" and 61 per cent of those in the South said, "Yes, I would object." When he repeated the same question two years later, the proportion of Southern parents who would object had dropped abruptly to 37 per cent. Similar, though less dramatic, changes were found in the attitudes of Northern parents. The millennium has scarcely arrived. Gallup went on to ask whether the parents would object to sending their children to a school where half, and then where more than half, of the children were colored. A majority of white parents in the North and almost four out of five of those in the South said they would object to the latter situation.

Certainly there is no evidence that the majority of American whites eagerly look forward to integration. Most are more comfortable in a segregated society, and they would prefer that the demonstrators slow down or go away while things are worked out more gradually. But most of them know also that racial discrimination is morally wrong and recognize the legitimacy of the Negro protest. Our survey data persuasively argue that where there is little or no protest against segregation and discrimination, or where these have the sanction of law, racial attitudes conform to the existing situation. But when attention is kept focused on racial injustice and when acts of discrimination become contrary to the law of the land, racial attitudes change. Conversely, there is no persuasive evidence thus far that either demonstrations and other forms of direct action, or legal sanctions applied by government, create a backlash effect and foster segregationist sentiment. On the contrary, they may simply demonstrate, ever more conclusively, that it is more costly to oppose integration than to bring it about. . . .

1. "America's Mood Today," *Look*, June 29, 1965; and Harris Survey news release, May 17, 1965.
2. Much of the material in this section has previously been presented in Herbert H. Hyman and Paul B. Sheatsley, "Attitudes Toward Desegregation," *Scientific American*, 211 (July 1964), 16–23.
3. The question was asked also in 1944 and 1946. Results for those years, while consistent with the trend, are not shown for reasons of space. Absence of financial support precluded asking the question on any other occasions, so we cannot conclude that the trend lines are uniformly smooth.
4. "South" refers to the South Atlantic, East South Central, and West South Central regions, as defined by the Bureau of the Census. "North" refers to the rest of the country, except Alaska and Hawaii, where no interviews were conducted.
5. The same holds true for the North. Northern whites living in segregated school areas were 65 per cent for integration, but in areas where there had been considerable integration, 83 per cent favored the policy.
6. In the 1956 and 1963 surveys, a special category was added for the response, "Yes, I would welcome it," and persons giving this reply were combined with the "No Difference" group.
7. We are indebted to Donald J. Treiman of the NORC staff for construction of this scale.
8. *Scientific American, op. cit.*

BREAKING THE VICIOUS CIRCLE

William Brink
Louis Harris

*Advocates of black separatism claim that blacks have abandoned
the idea of ultimate integration into the white society. They argue that
developing separate institutions, living in separate neighborhoods,
and being employed in separate firms would be preferable to integra-
tion. William Brink, of the* NEWSWEEK *editorial staff, and Louis
Harris, of Louis Harris and Associates, Inc., examine the results of
two recent opinion polls of Negro and white attitudes and opinions.
Neither the 1963 nor the 1966 poll indicates widespread support for
a separatist solution.*

Negroes do not want to take . . . things away from whites or to
destroy the white society that has them. On the contrary, Negroes ask
only for the chance to earn the better life with dignity.

To the Negro, one important dimension of dignity at work is in-
tegration on the job. By roughly 7 to 1, Negroes categorically stated
their preference for working in a mixed job force. Even in the South,
where such an experience has not been a common one, Negroes prefer
integration on the job by a 4 to 1 margin:

Negro Opinion on Integrated Jobs

	Total Rank and File %	Non-South %	South %
Prefer mixed group—			
Negroes and whites	76	84	68
Prefer mostly Negroes	11	6	17
Not sure	13	10	15

"Breaking the Vicious Circle" by William Brink and Louis Harris. From *The
Negro Revolution in America* (New York: Simon & Schuster, 1964), pp. 157–61.
Copyright © 1963 by Newsweek, Inc. Excerpted and reprinted by permission of
Simon & Schuster, Inc. and Louis Harris.

Negroes feel no less strongly about integrated education; again the margin in favor is 7 to 1. The way Negroes see it, the key to better education for their children is not to improve their own segregated schools but rather to integrate. Answering another question, Negro mothers said—by a better than 3 to 2 margin—that they would be willing to have their children picked up and transported to another part of town just to achieve integration.

A solid majority of Negroes everywhere in the country among the leadership group as well as the rank and file believe that Negro children will actually do better work if they go to school with whites.

Negroes seem to be convinced that integration in itself would have a salutary effect on their own children. To be sure, Negroes also believe that in mixed schools the present inferior facilities, equipment, textbooks and buildings would be eliminated. But fundamentally Negroes believe that segregation has a damaging effect on the psychological outlook of their children that can be rectified only through integration. In fact, the U.S. Supreme Court made precisely this point in its historic 1954 decision: "To separate them [children in grade and high schools] from others of similar age and qualifications solely because of their race generates a feeling of inferiority as to their status in the community that may affect their hearts and minds in a way unlikely ever to be undone."

When it comes to housing, Negroes are somewhat less sure about integration. Though the vast majority favor it, they do so with some trepidation. Many shared the feeling of a tool inspector in Philadelphia: "I wouldn't feel comfortable living with white people. I'm more at ease with my own people."

The following table reveals how Negroes feel about living in mixed or all-Negro neighborhoods:

Negro Opinion on Integrated Housing

	Total Rank and File %	Non-South %	South %
Prefer neighborhood with whites and Negroes	64	75	55
Prefer all-Negro neighborhood	20	11	27
Not sure	16	14	18

Three important facts should be noted about these results on housing. First, while Negroes feel, by a 7 to 1 margin that schools and employment should be integrated, the count drops to just over 3 to 1 for housing.

Second, even among the 64 per cent who say they want to integrate, nearly half add that it is not so much a matter of actually living next door to whites as having the right to do so. For example, Mrs. Eve B. de Lay, 49, a kindergarten teacher from New Orleans, put it this way: "I'm not eager to live among whites, but I feel that people should be able to live together in a neighborhood—if the whites don't move away."

The third important fact is that one-fifth of the Negroes prefer to live with their own. A 75-year-old woman in Cincinnati, Ohio, said, "I don't want to mix with white folks because they don't want to mix with me." A young textile worker from Sumter, South Carolina, added, in a switch that sounded like some whites talking about living in Negro neighborhoods: "I feel safer around Negroes." A house painter from Selma, North Carolina, saw only trouble between white and Negro children in a mixed neighborhood. "Because white young'uns are so mean and hard to get along with." A housewife from Pine Bluff, Arkansas, put it simply: "Because the old white devils pick at you so."

Ervin Abney, a Philadelphia construction worker, spoke for one Negro in every five when he said, "I'd get along better with my own kind. Some of them white people are hard to live around, if you know what I mean. Well, they'll act funny around you. They complain about things, take their kids away from yours, you know, things like that."

At the other end of the spectrum were Negroes who want to live in a white neighborhood because they do not particularly like living with people of their own race. A farmer in Biael Creek, North Carolina, for example, said, "I figure some whites treat you better than your own color will." A 54-year-old Chicago housewife finds Negroes objectionable this way: "Some of our colored people are terrible. The way they live, their mouths, their actions. When living with whites, you keep to yourself. The colored want to be sociable and some of them are terrible." Mrs. Lucy Howell, 59, of Memphis, Tennessee, differentiated between Negroes and "niggers" and added, "I don't like niggers." An unemployed man in Westchester County, New York, wanted to escape the whole problem: "I'd just like a half acre with nobody on it but me."

But the group who want integration in housing to avoid association with undesirable fellow Negroes is microscopic compared with those who feel that, as a matter of principle, integration is preferable. A 34-year-old unemployed woman in Providence, Rhode Island, put her finger on the psychological trauma of the ghetto: "I feel it isn't healthy to live in an all Negro area. In order to know people, it is necessary to mix. A number of Negroes made this point, emphasizing the importance of living in a mixed neighborhood *as a social experience* —particularly for their children. It was not merely a question of housing but of over-all personality development. A factory forelady in Philadelphia felt that associating with whites is part of growing up right: "I like my children to be able to associate with other types of children. I'd like for them to see how the other half lives." Mrs. Berlin Benson, a restaurant employee from Mt. Vernon, New York, underscored this feeling when she said, "I'd rather bring my children up in a white community. . . . They'd be able to cope with all situations. This way, being brought up only with Negroes, they don't learn how to cope with situations which might develop between Negroes and whites."

Other Negroes feel just as strongly that integrated housing is a necessity if whites are ultimately to accept them on equal terms. Mrs. Samuel Hill, a housewife in Wichita, Kansas, said, "I think I am intelligent enough to communicate with any of them. This is one of our largest problems." Another Mt. Vernon, New York, woman sees further lessons for whites in mixed housing: "It would make a better America. If they get to know us, they'd find out we don't all carry knives and are just as good as they. In fact, I know some I feel I am better than they are."

One Negro in every twenty reported having lived in mixed neighborhoods—and most of these liked the experience. An office cleaner in Cleveland, Ohio, reported, "The white neighbors that I have always known have always been very nice to my family." A Woodville, Mississippi, construction worker added, "I live close to white families now and we get along O.K." A 43-year-old butcher from St. Louis found his neighborhood turning black and regretted it: "I've found that it is pretty nice to live around mixed neighborhoods. When I first came here, it wasn't nothing but white and it was a nicer neighborhood."

The reason almost two out of every three Negroes prefer integrated housing is not the superior facilities of white neighborhoods. Rather, it is more the psychological effect of liberation from the ghetto and the deeply felt desire to prove to whites that Negroes aren't as bad as they think.

How soon and how fast will this liberation take place? The vicious circle argues against it happening soon. Indeed, Negroes themselves believe it may come slower than many whites now fear. When asked to give their estimate of just how much integration they expect to take place in the next five years, only a minority of Negroes though it would be extensive:

Negro Estimate of Integration in the Next Five Years

	Total Rank and File %	South %	Non-South %
A lot of integration	33	34	34
Some, not a lot of integration	36	38	33
Only a little integration	17	18	17
Not sure	14	10	16

These results point clearly to the fact that Negroes do not expect the millennium overnight.

The next question, and a key one, is: just what does the word "integration" mean for them? Does it mean a massive outpouring of Negroes from their ghettos into white suburbs, schools, restaurants, social organizations and churches? The Negro's own answer is that this is not his primary or immediate goal. What he wants now is to be treated as a human being; and part and parcel of this is the *right* to integrate.

Negroes were specifically asked to choose which was more important to them—equal treatment or "a lot of mixing of the races." By a margin of better than 8 to 1 they chose equal treatment.

SUPPLEMENTARY STATISTICAL TABLES

William Brink
Louis Harris

2(e) At work, would you rather work alongside mostly other Negroes, or would you rather work with a mixed group of whites and Negroes?

	Total all inter- views		Total non- South		Total South		South Urban		Non- urban		Negro com- munity leaders
	1966 %	1963 %	1966 %	1963 %	1966 %	1963 %	1966 %	1963 %	1966 %	1963 %	1966 %
Mostly other Negroes	10	11	6	6	13	17	8	14	18	22	6
Mixed group	80	76	86	84	75	68	81	72	69	63	51
Not sure	10	13	8	10	12	15	11	14	13	15	43

5(a) In living in a neighborhood, if you could find the housing you want and like, would you rather live in a neighborhood with Negro families, or in a neighborhood that had both whites and Negroes?

"Supplementary Statistical Tables" by William Brink and Louis Harris. From *Black and White* (New York: Simon & Schuster, 1967), Appendix D, pp. 232–35. Copyright © 1968, 1967 by Newsweek, Inc. Excerpted and reprinted by permission of Simon & Schuster, Inc.

	Total all interviews		Total non-South		Total South		South				Negro community leaders
							Urban		Non-urban		
	1966 %	1963 %	1966 %	1963 %	1966 %	1963 %	1966 %	1963 %	1966 %	1963 %	1966 %
Negroes	17	20	8	11	26	27	22	26	29	33	10
Whites and Negroes	68	64	79	75	57	55	58	57	56	50	59
Not sure	15	16	13	14	17	18	20	17	15	17	31

6(b) Would you like to see all Negro children in your family go to school with white children or not?

	Total all interviews		Total non-South		Total South		South				Negro community leaders
							Urban		Non-urban		
	1966 %	1963 %	1966 %	1963 %	1966 %	1963 %	1966 %	1963 %	1966 %	1963 %	1966 %
Go with whites	70	70	82	79	60	63	70	66	51	58	69
Not go with whites	11	10	5	7	16	12	13	10	19	16	4
Not sure	19	20	13	14	24	25	17	24	30	26	27

PART V

Alternative Policies

RECOMMENDATIONS FOR NATIONAL ACTION

The Kerner Commission

The National Advisory Commission on Civil Disorders escaped the obscurity of most Presidential commissions with its charge of white racism and its finding that America is moving toward two societies— separate and unequal. To reverse these trends they proposed a large-scale and diverse attack on the problems of American society. Their recommendations for national action are summarized under three main headings: employment, education, and housing.

Introduction

No American—white or black—can escape the consequences of the continuing social and economic decay of our major cities.

Only a commitment to national action on an unprecedented scale can shape a future compatible with the historic ideals of American society.

The great productivity of our economy, and a Federal revenue system which is highly responsive to economic growth, can provide the resources.

The major need is to generate new will—the will to tax ourselves to the extent necessary to meet the vital needs of the Nation.

We have set forth goals and proposed strategies to reach those goals. We discuss and recommend programs not to commit each of us to specific parts of such programs, but to illustrate the type and dimension of action needed.

The major goal is the creation of a true union—a single society and a single American identity. Toward that goal, we propose the following objectives for national action:

"Recommendations for National Action." From the *Summary of the Report of the National Advisory Commission on Civil Disorders* (Washington, D.C.: Government Printing Office, March, 1968), pp. 11–13.

Opening up opportunities to those who are restricted by racial segregation and discrimination, and eliminating all barriers to their choice of jobs, education, and housing.

Removing the frustration of powerlessness among the disadvantaged by providing the means for them to deal with the problems that affect their own lives and by increasing the capacity of our public and private institutions to respond to these problems.

Increasing communication across racial lines to destroy stereotypes, halt polarization, end distrust and hostility, and create common ground for efforts toward public order and social justice.

We propose these aims to fulfill our pledge of equality and to meet the fundamental needs of a democratic and civilized society—domestic peace and social justice.

Employment

Pervasive unemployment and underemployment are the most persistent and serious grievances in minority areas. They are inextricably linked to the problem of civil disorder.

Despite growing Federal expenditures for manpower development and training programs, and sustained general economic prosperity and increasing demands for skilled workers, about 2 million—white and nonwhite—are permanently unemployed. About 10 million are underemployed, of whom 6.5 million work full time for wages below the poverty line.

The 500,000 "hard-core" unemployed in the central cities who lack a basic education and are unable to hold a steady job are made up in large part of Negro males between the ages of 18 and 25. In the riot cities which we surveyed, Negroes were three times as likely as whites to hold unskilled jobs, which are often part time, seasonal, low paying and "dead end."

Negro males between the ages of 15 and 25 predominated among the rioters. More than 20 per cent of the rioters were unemployed, and many who were employed held intermittent, low status, unskilled jobs which they regarded as below their education and ability.

The Commission recommends that the Federal Government:

Undertake joint efforts with cities and states to consolidate existing manpower programs to avoid fragmentation and duplication.

Take immediate action to create 2 million new jobs over the next 3 years—1 million in the public sector and 1 million in the private sector —to absorb the hard-core unemployed and materially reduce the level of underemployment for all workers, black and white. We propose 250,000 public sector and 300,000 private sector jobs in the first year.

Provide on-the-job training by both public and private employers with reimbursement to private employers for the extra costs of training the hard-core unemployed, by contract or by tax credits.

Provide tax and other incentives to investment in rural as well as urban poverty areas in order to offer to the rural poor an alternative to migration to urban centers.

Take new and vigorous action to remove artificial barriers to employment and promotion, including not only racial discrimination but, in certain cases, arrest records or lack of a high school diploma. Strengthen those agencies such as the Equal Employment Opportunity Commission, charged with eliminating discriminatory practices, and provide full support for Title VI of the 1964 Civil Rights Act allowing Federal grant-in-aid funds to be withheld from activities which discriminate on grounds of color or race.

The Commission commends the recent public commitment of the National Council of the Building and Construction Trades Unions, AFL-CIO, to encourage and recruit Negro membership in apprentice-ship programs. This commitment should be intensified and imple-mented.

Education

Education in a democratic society must equip children to develop their potential and to participate fully in American life. For the com-munity at large, the schools have discharged this responsibility well. But for many minorities, and particularly for the children of the ghetto, the schools have failed to provide the educational experience which could overcome the effects of discrimination and deprivation.

This failure is one of the persistent sources of grievance and resent-ment within the Negro community. The hostility of Negro parents and students toward the school system is generating increasing conflict and causing disruption within many city school districts. But the most dramatic evidence of the relationship between educational practices and civil disorders lies in the high incidence of riot participation by ghetto youth who have not completed high school.

The bleak record of public education for ghetto children is grow-ing worse. In the critical skills—verbal and reading ability—Negro students are falling further behind whites with each year of school completed. The high unemployment and underemployment rate for Negro youth is evidence, in part, of the growing educational crisis.

We support integration as the priority education strategy; it is es-sential to the future of American society. In this last summer's disorders we have seen the consequences of racial isolation at all levels, and of attitudes toward race, on both sides, produced by three centuries of myth, ignorance, and bias. It is indispensable that opportunities for in-teraction between the races be expanded.

We recognize that the growing dominance of pupils from disad-vantaged minorities in city school populations will not soon be reversed. No matter how great the effort toward desegregation, many children of the ghetto will not, within their school careers, attend integrated schools.

If existing disadvantages are not to be perpetuated, we must drastically improve the quality of ghetto education. Equality of results with all-white schools must be the goal.

To implement these strategies, the Commission recommends:

Sharply increased efforts to eliminate de facto segregation in our schools through substantial federal aid to school systems seeking to desegregate either within the system or in cooperation with neighboring school systems.

Elimination of racial discrimination in Northern as well as Southern schools by vigorous application of Title VI of the Civil Rights Act of 1964.

Extension of quality early childhood education to every disadvantaged child in the country.

Efforts to improve dramatically schools serving disadvantaged children through substantial federal funding of year-round quality compensatory education programs, improved teaching, and expanded experimentation and research.

Elimination of illiteracy through greater Federal support for adult basic education.

Enlarged opportunities for parent and community participation in the public schools.

Reoriented vocational education emphasizing work-experience training and the involvement of business and industry.

Expanded opportunities for higher education through increased federal assistance to disadvantaged students.

Revision of state aid formulas to assure more per student aid to districts having a high proportion of disadvantaged school age children.

The Welfare System

Our present system of public welfare is designed to save money instead of people, and tragically ends up doing neither. This system has two critical deficiencies:

First, it excludes large numbers of persons who are in great need, and who, if provided a decent level of support, might be able to become more productive and self-sufficient. No Federal funds are available for millions of unemployed and underemployed men and women who are needy but neither aged, handicapped nor the parents of minor children.

Second, for those included, the system provides assistance well below the minimum necessary for a decent level of existence, and imposes restrictions that encourage continued dependency on welfare and undermine self-respect.

A welter of statutory requirements and administrative practices and regulations operate to remind recipients that they are considered untrustworthy, promiscuous, and lazy. Residence requirements prevent assistance to people in need who are newly arrived in the state. Searchers of recipients' homes violate privacy. Inadequate social services compound the problems.

The Commission recommends that the Federal Government, acting with state and local governments where necessary, reform the existing welfare system to:

Establish, for recipients in existing welfare categories, uniform national standards of assistance at least as high as the annual "poverty level" of income, now set by the Social Security Administration at $3,335 per year for an urban family of four.

Require that all states receiving Federal welfare contributions participate in the Aid to Families with Dependent Children-Unemployed Parents Program (AFDC–UP) that permits assistance to families with both father and mother in the home, thus aiding the family while it is still intact.

Bear a substantially greater portion of all welfare costs—at least 90 per cent of total payments.

Increase incentives for seeking employment and job training, but remove restrictions recently enacted by the Congress that would compel mothers of young children to work.

Provide more adequate social services through neighborhood centers and family-planning program.

Remove the freeze placed by the 1967 welfare amendments on the percentage of children in a State that can be covered by Federal assistance.

Eliminate residence requirements.

As a long-range goal, the Commission recommends that the Federal Government seek to develop a national system of income supplementation based strictly on need with two broad and basic purposes:

To provide, for those who can work or who do work, any necessary supplements in such a way as to develop incentives for fuller employment.

To provide, for those who cannot work and for mothers who decide to remain with their children, a minimum standard of decent living, and to aid in saving children from the prison of poverty that has held their parents.

A broad system of supplementation would involve substantially greater Federal expenditures than anything now contemplated. The cost will range widely depending on the standard of need accepted as the "basic allowance" to individuals and families, and on the rate at which additional income above this level is taxed. Yet if the deepening cycle of poverty and dependence on welfare can be broken, if the children of the poor can be given the opportunity to scale the wall that now separates them from the rest of society, the return on this investment will be great indeed.

Housing

After more than three decades of fragmented and grossly under-funded Federal housing programs, nearly 6 million substandard housing units remain occupied in the United States.

The housing problem is particularly acute in the minority ghettos. Nearly two-thirds of all nonwhite families living in the central cities today live in neighborhoods marked by substandard housing and general urban blight. Two major factors are responsible:

First: Many ghetto residents simply cannot pay the rent necessary to support decent housing. In Detroit, for example, over 40 per cent of the nonwhite-occupied units in 1960 required rent of over 35 per cent of the tenants' income.

Second: Discrimination prevents access to many nonslum areas, particularly the suburbs, where good housing exists. In addition, by creating a "back pressure" in the racial ghettos, it makes it possible for landlords to break up apartments for denser occupancy, and keeps prices and rents of deteriorated ghetto housing higher than they would be in a truly free market.

To date, Federal programs have been able to do comparatively little to provide housing for the disadvantaged. In the 31-year history of subsidized Federal housing, only about 800,000 units have been constructed, with recent production averaging about 50,000 units a year. By comparison, over a period only 3 years longer, FHA insurance guarantees have made possible the construction of over 10 million middle and upper income units.

Two points are fundamental to the Commission's recommendations:

First: Federal housing programs must be given a new thrust aimed at overcoming the prevailing patterns of racial segregation. If this is not done, those programs will continue to concentrate the most impoverished and dependent segments of the population into the central-city ghettos where there is already a critical gap between the needs of the population and the public resources to deal with them.

Second: The private sector must be brought into the production and financing of low and moderate-rental housing to supply the capabilities and capital necessary to meet the housing needs of the Nation.

The Commission recommends that the Federal Government:

Enact a comprehensive and enforceable Federal open-housing law to cover the sale or rental of all housing, including single-family homes.

Reorient Federal housing programs to place more low- and moderate-income housing outside of ghetto areas.

Bring within the reach of low- and moderate-income families within the next 5 years 6 million new and existing units of decent housing, beginning with 600,000 units in the next year.

To reach this goal we recommend:

Expansion and modification of the rent supplement program to permit use of supplements for existing housing, thus greatly increasing the reach of the program.

Expansion and modification of the below-market interest rate program to enlarge the interest subsidy to all sponsors, provide interest-free loans to nonprofit sponsors to cover preconstruction costs, and permit sale of projects to nonprofit corporations, co-operatives, or condominiums.

Creation of an ownership supplement program similar to present rent supplements, to make home ownership possible for low-income families.

Federal writedown of interest rates on loans to private builders constructing moderate-rent housing.

Expansion of the public housing program, with emphasis on small units on scattered sites, and leasing and "turnkey" programs.

Expansion of the Model Cities program.

Expansion and reorientation of the urban renewal program to give priority to projects directly assisting low-income households to obtain adequate housing.

CONCLUSION

One of the first witnesses to be invited to appear before this Commission was Dr. Kenneth B. Clark, a distinguished and perceptive scholar. Referring to the reports of earlier riot commissions, he said:

I read that report . . . of the 1919 riot in Chicago, and it is as if I were reading the report of the investigating committee on the Harlem riot of '35, the report of the investigating committee on the Harlem riot of '43, the report of the McCone Commission on the Watts riot.

I must again in candor say to you members of this Commission—it is a kind of Alice in Wonderland—with the same moving picture reshown over and over again, the same analysis, the same recommendations, and the same inaction.

These words come to our minds as we conclude this report.

We have provided an honest beginning. We have learned much. But we have uncovered no startling truths, no unique insights, no simple solutions. The destruction and the bitterness of racial disorder, the harsh polemics of black revolt and white repression have been seen and heard before in this country.

It is time now to end the destruction and the violence, not only in the streets of the ghetto but in the lives of people.

INDUSTRIAL INVESTMENT
IN URBAN POVERTY AREAS

Robert F. Kennedy

*The late Senator Robert F. Kennedy was one of the most aggressive
proponents of legislation to improve the economic position of blacks.
He was the author of a number of proposals and bills designed to
encourage profit-making firms to invest in the ghetto. This excerpt
from one of his speeches outlines his bill to encourage industrial
investment in urban poverty areas and presents the rationale for these
measures.*

I rise for the purpose of introducing . . . a bill for private invest-
ment in urban, poverty areas . . .

The specific purpose of the bill is to stimulate investment—the
creation of new jobs and income—in poverty areas. The entire program
is to be carried out, not by Government agencies, but by private en-
terprise. The Federal Government provides only a system of tax incen-
tives, carefully designed to enable private enterprise to make its in-
vestments and carry out its operations in the urban poverty areas.

Thus the bill seeks to remedy the greatest failure in our existing
poverty efforts: the failure to involve and rely on the private enter-
prise system which is the basic strength of the Nation. By failing to
involve the private sector, we have not only ignored the potential con-
tribution of millions of talented and energetic Americans in tens of
thousands of productive enterprises. More dangerously, we have
created for the poor a separate economy, almost a separate nation: a
second rate system of welfare handouts, a screen of Government
agencies keeping the poor apart from the rest of us. That system—in-
effective, inefficient, and degrading—must be changed. This bill would
work toward the needed change.

From a speech to the United States Senate by Senator Robert F. Kennedy
printed in the *Congressional Record* on July 12, 1967.

In brief summary, the program will work as follows: An enterprise wishing to avail itself of the bill's provisions will select a site in a poverty area, in cooperation with the city and Federal Government, and the local community affected. The company will agree to create at least 50 new jobs; to fill at least two-thirds of all jobs at this location with residents of the poverty area—or other unemployed persons —and to maintain its investment for at least 10 years. In return, it will receive tax credits against its investment in plant and machinery; accelerated depreciation schedules for that investment; extra deductions for wages paid to previously unemployed persons; liberal carryforward and carryback allowances and assistance in training the new workers.

After extensive consultation with representatives of business, labor, government, the academic community, and the urban poor themselves, our expectation is that these incentives will give our private enterprise system—the most ingenious and productive the world has ever known—the help it needs to effectively attack the difficult and resistant problems of urban unemployment.

Because it operates through the existing private enterprise system, the bill does not require the creation of new Government departments or agencies. It creates no new systems of welfare handouts. It requires no great new outflows of Government spending. Rather, by generating new investment and creating new jobs, it will increase productivity in the Nation as a whole—putting idle hands to work, turning welfare recipients into taxpayers, and decreasing present financial burdens on State and local governments. And greater productivity will result, in our judgment, in increased overall Federal revenues, even after allowing for the tax relief afforded to businesses which make the desired investment.

I. THE NEED FOR JOBS

This Nation faces many problems. . . . But of all our problems, none is more immediate—none is more pressing—none is more omnipresent—than the crisis of unemployment in every major city in the Nation.

*   *   *

II. THE NEED FOR PRIVATE ENTERPRISE PARTICIPATION

In the last 7 years, we have tried to solve this terrible problem. Almost every Congress has enacted another bill designed to put people to work: the Area Redevelopment Act, the Manpower Development and Training Act, the Investment Credit Act, the Economic Development Act; and the landmark Elementary and Secondary Education Act, to provide the educational base which is often so sadly neglected. But . . . the test is results: whether we in fact achieve true equality of opportunity for all our people. And by that test, our past measures, necessary and effective as they have often been, have not been adequate to the urban crisis. For the fact that despite all our efforts, despite the uninterrupted rise in prosperity experienced by the rest of the Nation these past 7 years, the 1967 manpower report states flatly that:

Economic and social conditions are getting worse, not better, in slum areas.

* * *

Many analysts have tried to explain why our present efforts have failed to provide adequate employment for the poverty areas. The Subcommittee on Executive Reorganization heard dozens of witnesses with varying answers; and certainly all agreed that there is no single cause—that improved programs for education, for political organization, for training, for housing, all must play their part.

But if there is one single shortcoming, one thing we have done hardly at all, it is to enlist the energies and resources and talents of private enterprise in this most urgent national effort. Our training programs, our educational programs, our poverty programs, our housing programs —all these have been Government-financed, and most have been Government run. They have been designed in Washington. Their funds have been voted by appropriation. Their implementation has been through Government agencies existing or newly created. I have supported these efforts, and called for their expansion. I have believed, and continue to believe, that while improvement in their organization and function is needed, they are often worthwhile and necessary, and deserve far greater support than they now receive. But their strongest advocate must admit that they are not enough.

To rely exclusively, even primarily, on government efforts is not only to ignore the shaping traditions of American life and politics. To ignore the potential contribution of private enterprise is to fight the war on poverty with a single platoon, while great armies are left to stand aside. For private enterprise is not just another part of America; in a significant sense, private enterprise is the very sinew and strength of America. Our productive assets, our machines and money and plants are owned by private enterprise. The entire intricate chain of the economy—the means by which we join with our fellows to produce goods and roads, to bring food to our tables and clothes to our backs—all this is organized by private enterprise. Private enterprise has built our cities, and industries; it has created jobs for over 60 million Americans now at work. But it has not rebuilt the centers of poverty, nor put their people to work. And in my judgment, the lack of private enterprise participation is the principal cause for our failure to solve the problem of employment in urban poverty areas.

It is not for want of a sense of responsibility, nor out of willful ignorance, that private enterprise has not played its full role. The Subcommittee on Executive Reorganization heard from many businessmen aware of the challenge and eager to meet it. . . .

And in recent months, I have talked with other businessmen and academicians, labor leaders and city planners. Almost unanimously, they have agreed on two related propositions. First, private enterprise must invest its resources in poverty areas. Second, it must receive assistance from Government to do so. . . .

Private corporations, after all, are responsible to their stockholders. Large-scale investment in poverty areas will certainly be more costly and difficult than investment elsewhere; that, after all, is why investment has not taken place in these areas in the past. Land, transportation, insurance against fire and vandalism, training of workers, extra supervision—all these are so costly in poverty areas as to make investment there, under present conditions, uneconomical. If private enterprise is to play its full part in poverty areas, therefore, it must have the support of Government to help make up for the increased costs.

III. PRIVATE ENTERPRISE PARTICIPATION: THE MECHANICS

In what way should private enterprise now be encouraged to join the fight against unemployment? For us, the answer is simple and direct: it should create new jobs, and train and hire unemployed and poor people to fill them. The actual creation of new jobs is the single greatest lack in present programs. And the lack of job opportunities handicaps all other efforts. Education programs are hurt when students see their fathers and older brothers idle; if no jobs are waiting, they ask, why bother with education? The same lack of jobs has caused high dropout rates from job-training programs. Housing programs suffer when unemployment causes overcrowding. The need is for jobs and income, now. And the creation of new jobs, new productive enterprise, is the task that private business can and must undertake.

The next question is where these jobs should be created. Our answer is that to have a maximum impact on the problems of the urban poor, the new enterprises must be established, the new jobs must be created, in the urban poverty areas. There are four principal reasons for so limiting the choice of sites.

First, we know that at the present time, large numbers of the urban poor cannot be induced to take jobs away from the areas in which they live. Secretary of Labor Willard Wirtz told the Executive Reorganization Subcommittee that "most of the unemployed in the slums" are so "conditioned by a century of insecurity" that even distances of "more than six or eight blocks away from where they live" create a severe problem; and most new job openings are, of course, much more than a few blocks outside poverty areas.

Second, even if we could induce the urban poor to commute to jobs far outside their areas, most cities lack the mass transportation facilities to take them to and from their place of work at a price they can afford to pay. . . . Nor is inexpensive housing available, or likely soon to be available, near the new job openings that do exist.

Third, the location of new industrial facilities in urban poverty areas will have an important "multiplier" effect on the creation of jobs. New auxiliary businesses will be spunoff in the same area to service the needs of the primary facility. New retail and service facilities—restaurants and food stores, barbershops, dry cleaners, and clothing stores— will be required to satisfy the demands of the workers at the primary establishment. Depending upon the area, I have received estimates that for every three jobs created in a primary facility, from two to three additional jobs may be created in secondary and service facilities nearby. Each of these derivative jobs and entrepreneurial opportunities will be open to poverty area residents, without further Government action.

Fourth, location of investment and jobs within poverty areas is important for its own sake. Partly, it is important to end these areas' isolation—to bring not just individual residents, but the entire community, back into contact with the mainstream of American life. For another part, it is important that children and young people see change and development take place through the work of their own fathers and brothers—providing concrete hope through living example. And for another part, it is vital that poverty areas, like other communities, be able to develop a sense of joint community achievement and purpose.

This is not to say that this Nation need not strive for an open society, in which the residents of poverty areas, and in particular residents of the Negro ghetto, who have achieved financial and social security, have complete freedom to choose where they will live and work. That is birthright for all of us; and it must be achieved. But I believe that it is far more important that the vast majority of our urban poor be enabled to achieve basic financial stability and a sense of dignity and security where they live now. That is the indispensable first step toward the full freedom of citizenship.

IV. INCENTIVES

To encourage the creation of new enterprise, the investment of capital in urban poverty areas, we require an adequate system of incentives. To devise such a system, I have talked with economists, tax experts, city planners, and business leaders alike. Their expert knowledge, and previous experience . . . leads to the conclusion that the most simple, efficient, and effective vehicle for encouraging such investment is the enactment of a system of tax incentives.

The concept of government incentives to induce desired investments by private industry is neither new nor radical. Rather it is a concept honored by practice since the founding of the Republic. From 1792 until well into the 1830's, the bulk of Federal expenditure was devoted to creating and inducing internal improvements, particularly the roads and canals which opened up new territory for settlement. Throughout the 19th century, Government induced the building of railroads, including the great transcontinental roads, by offering liberal grants of land on either side of the right-of-way; . . . In this century, similar practices have extended into every corner of our economy.

Even more than with such direct inducements we have used the tax laws as a means of persuading private citizens and enterprises to invest in desired ways, at desired times, and in desired locations. To encourage long-term investment, we tax capital gains at half the normal rate. To encourage charitable contributions, we allow them to be deducted from current income. To encourage oil and mineral production, we offer depletion allowances. To encourage the building of grain-storage facilities and defense plants, we have offered faster-than-normal depreciation rates. To encourage investment in capital goods as opposed to inventory or consumption, we have allowed tax credits for such investment; suspended that credit when we wished to slow investment down; and, just recently reinstated it in order to speed investment up again.

The principle that the tax code may be used to induce certain investment applies to questions of investment location as well as to the fact of investment. . . .

That such tax incentives can prove effective in attracting investment capital is demonstrated by Puerto Rico's Operation Bootstrap. There, a system of tax exemptions, carefully protected by our own Internal Revenue Code, has helped just since 1948 to set up over 1,100 plants and factories. Manufacturing income has increased by more than 600 per cent; per capita income has risen 300 per cent; the number of workers engaged in manufacturing has almost tripled. The economy of this little island has grown at an annual rate of over 9 per cent—

a rate which far surpasses the economic growth of the United States as a whole.

Of course, exceptional tax incentives should not be lightly given. Any exception and departure from a uniform tax base should be required to meet two tests. First . . . we must ask if the provision will "promote desirable social or economic objectives of overriding importance." Second, if certain preferential tax treatment is to be given to certain members of a class, then we must be sure that these benefits are not creating a special, privileged group, but are only compensating for additional risks and burdens. . . .

In my judgment, tax incentives for investment in ghetto areas meet both of these criteria. Certainly they will promote a "desirable objective" of "overriding importance"—the employment and self-sufficiency of American citizens, and the improvement of conditions in our most important cities. Moreover, they are fair. They insure nothing more than a reasonable return to those who will face the higher costs and the labor problems involved in establishing facilities within ghetto areas; they do no more than compensate business for the costs and uncertainties of remedial training, difficult transportation, possible vandalism or fire damage, and extra executive time and effort.

V. THE BILL

The bill . . . builds upon all of these past experiments. Its objective is to foster a partnership between private industry, the Federal Government, and our major cities in coping with the unemployment which scars and cripples the urban poverty area. To accomplish this objective, the bill provides:

First. The various incentives will apply not to relocating businesses, but only to companies which will construct new facilities, or expand existing ones, in urban poverty areas. In short, it will create new jobs.

*   *   *

Second. Those cities, encompassing urban poverty areas, which decide to participate in the program—and it shall be a matter of individual choice for each city— . . . will determine new industrial investment within its poverty areas.

Third. . . . The bill also provides, as a safeguard against insubstantial or fly-by-night operators, that the facility must employ a minimum total of 50 workers—reduced to 25 in cities of under 50,000 persons and on Indian reservations. But if a lower minimum is found to be an adequate safeguard, I would favor that lower requirement, in order to attract the participation of as wide a segment of American business as possible.

Fourth. The only qualifying businesses shall be those which will hire a significant number of unskilled or semiskilled workers and which do not directly compete with local entrepreneurs; the bill covers manufacturers, producers, and distributors, but does not apply to any retailers. . . . Its provisions also cover construction firms that will locate in urban poverty areas, hire local workers, and engage in construction within those areas.

Fifth. The working force hired by the qualifying employer will be trained under the auspices of the Department of Labor. Such training . . . will be aimed at giving specific individuals the skills to fill specific positions. The acual training will be done either by local agencies, or by the employer himself, who will receive funds to cover his costs from the Department of Labor. . . .

Sixth. Any qualifying business shall receive the following tax incentives during the 10 years immediately following the time that it begins operations:

A 10-per cent credit on machinery and equipment, in lieu of the normal maximum 7-per cent credit.

A 7-per cent credit on expenditures for constructing an industrial facility or for leasing space for a qualifying business.

A credit carryback of 3 taxable years and a carryover of 10 taxable years.

A useful life, for purposes of depreciation, of 66⅔ per cent of the normal useful life applicable to real and personal property.

A net operating loss carryover of 10 taxable years.

A special deduction of an additional 25 per cent of the salaries paid to all workers hired to meet the requirements of this act.

Three characteristics of these incentives are worthy of particular attention.

First, they are carefully directed at the particular problem of investment in poverty areas. The existing tax credit for machinery is extended to facility construction, to allow for the fact that most enterprises will have to build new facilities, rather than simply expand existing facilities. The carryover and carryback provisions are lengthened to 10 years, to allow for the likelihood that a development of profits will take longer than usual. The special deduction for wages and salaries will encourage intensive use of labor, thus putting relatively more men to work, as opposed to machinery, in relation to a given volume of production.

Second, these provisions are drafted so as to introduce a minimum of new complexity into the Internal Revenue Code. . . .

Third, they will be effective. Investment credits and accelerated depreciation, and the other elements of this system, have proven their ability to stimulate new investment both in Europe and in the United States. George Terborgh of the Machinery and Allied Products Institute has estimated that the existing tax credit, together with a 15-per cent reduction in useful life for depreciation purposes, afford about a 20-per cent increase in the normal rate of return. The extended tax credit in this bill, together with the 33-per cent reduction in useful life, would double that increase if available outside poverty areas; in the conditions under which they will actually be available, for investment in poverty areas, these incentives should produce a return at least equivalent to that under the most favorable conditions outside these areas.

Seventh. If the qualified business fails to hold its real or personal property for stipulated periods of 10 and 4 years respectively then all credits allowed for expenditures on this property shall be recovered by the Treasury.

*   *   *

VI. COSTS AND BENEFITS

Any proposal for tax credits and deductions should be carefully considered with respect to its cost. Will there be a revenue loss? Or will costs be more than made up by the benefits?

I believe that this bill will in fact pay for itself; that it will not result in a net revenue loss. Rather, if successful, it will bring substantial benefits to the Treasury, to State and local governments, to the economy in general—and to tens of thousands of individual Americans.

It is of course impossible to estimate with any precision the extent to which businessmen and firms will take advantage of these incentives; that will be the product of thousands of individual business decisions. But what can be clearly demonstrated, I believe, is that to whatever extent the bill is used, the result will be a net benefit to the Treasury, and to the Nation. To make this demonstration, we can analyze a hypothetical case of a single business firm under the bill; but recognizing that these calculations are themselves only rough approximations, we will err on the side of conservatism.

Assume, then, a firm which invests $1 million in a poverty-area enterprise, split equally between plant and equipment. The tax credit allowed against the plant will be 7 per cent, or $35,000. Against the equipment, under law now in effect, an average credit of about 5 per cent would be allowed. Under this bill, a 10 per cent credit would be allowed—an increase of 5 per cent, or $25,000. The total tax credit would be $85,000; the credit attributable to this bill, $60,000.

Assume further that this investment creates 50 new jobs. This is, in fact, a very conservative assumption, since the Department of Commerce informs me that the average production job now requires about $11,000 in capital investment; we are allowing, for this hypothetical analysis, a very expensive $20,000 investment to create each new job. At any rate, 50 new jobs, at a conservative $5,000 per job annual wage, would represent a total annual payroll of $250,000. Against this payroll, the employer would take the bill's additional 25-per cent deduction on wages paid to poverty area residents. Thus, even if all the new jobs were filled by such residents, his maximum savings, at current corporate tax rates, would be about $31,000.

On the other hand, the Federal Government would collect on this payroll a minimum of $30,000 in individual income taxes. Its revenues would be further increased by taxes on the profits of the firms which built the plant and machinery, and sold it to the hypothetical businessman; assuming their profit at 10 per cent before taxes, this extra investment would bring the Treasury an additional $50,000. Now let us recall that for every three jobs created directly by this bill, it is estimated that from two to three additional jobs will be created indirectly; and let us assume conservatively that in this case, only one job will be created indirectly for every two jobs created directly. This would mean another 25 new jobs without Government assistance. Assuming that these would be lower paying jobs—say, only $4,000 a year each—they would produce an additional payroll of $100,000; of which the Federal Government would receive a minimum of $10,000 in income taxes.

Finally, assume that in the absence of these new jobs for 75 men, the families of only 10 would receive Federal aid-to-dependent-children payments. In most urban areas, these 10 families would cost the Federal Government at least $25,000 a year; in cities like New York, the cost would be much greater. Adding the welfare saving to the increased tax collections, we find that the Federal Government has gained a total of $115,000 in the first year alone—more than matching the $91,000 of tax savings received by the businessman.

Of course, this calculation is far from exact, and it is not comprehensive. It does not allow for the effect of accelerated depreciation. It does not allow for the continuing cost of the excess wage deductions in future years. But it also does not allow for the additional taxes the Federal Treasury will collect as a result of the purchases of the newly hired workers. It does not allow for the tax collections which will accompany the business profits on the secondary jobs created, or on the general attendant increase in economic activity. It does not count increased tax collections at the State and local level, nor for the increased tax base which may alleviate property tax burdens in the municipalities. It does not allow for income taxes collected in future years, which will rise as the workers' incomes rise. And the hypothetical case makes no allowance for taxes on any profit which the business may make. All these will add to, not detract from, Government revenues.

It may be asked, are these calculations dependent on the assumption that the investment receiving tax credits would not have taken place except for the incentives. Thus after the enactment of the 1962 tax credit, it was estimated that most of the investment receiving its benefits would have taken place in any case; and the benefits of the 1962 credit were assertedly diluted. Even allowing for this dilution, Secretary of the Treasury Dillon estimated that the 1962 credit repaid half its value to the Treasury just in the first year of its operation. But the tax incentives of this bill are far more narrowly drawn than were those of 1962; and its benefits will be far less subject to dilution.

*   *   *

Now let us remember again that the 1962 act, notwithstanding its more general applicability, still returned half its benefits to the Treasury in its first year. I think there is no question that this more precisely focused bill will, within a very short time, repay more than its full value to the Government.

*   *   *

VII. CONCLUSION

This bill will not solve the problems of poverty. But it will help. It will not educate children—but it will give their fathers jobs, and their families income, and thus help create a family atmosphere in which education can more easily take place. The bill will not cure disease—but it will help provide the incomes to buy better food, and decent living conditions, and to pay for decent medical care. It will not comfort the old, or banish discrimination, or create by itself a sense of community in the city. But it will engage the energies and resources of a nation, as they have not been engaged before, in a new partnership against poverty; a partnership of government and its people, business and labor and the poor themselves.

CAPITAL IN THE GHETTOS

Richard M. Nixon

During the Presidential campaign of 1968 the concept of "black capitalism" became a popular response to the disappointment associated with the antipoverty program. Candidate Richard M. Nixon, calling for "new approaches" to the problems of the cities, proposed a broad range of tax incentives and guaranteed loans to encourage private industry to locate in ghetto areas. He stated: "What we have to do is to get private enterprise into the ghetto and get the people of the ghetto into private enterprise . . ."

When we think of the urban crisis, we think first of the problems of race and poverty—which too often go hand in hand.

To the problems of poverty, many reply: provide government jobs, government housing, government welfare. Government has a role. But what government can do best is to provide the incentives to get *private* resources and energies where the need is. What we need today is not more millions on welfare rolls but more millions on payrolls.

Thus, for example, in the area of jobs I have proposed such measures as tax credits for businesses to hire and train the unemployed: a national computer job bank, to bring job-seeking men and man-seeking jobs together; and special tax incentives to businesses that locate branch offices or new plants in poverty areas.

A few years ago, American industry was given a 7 per cent tax credit for the modernization of equipment. The credits were widely used. Productivity increased, and the entire economy benefitted. A similar tax credit for increasing the productivity of people is overdue, and along with it should go a vigorous effort—led by the President— to persuade industry to utilize it to the fullest. Workers, business, and the nation would benefit.

"Capital in the Ghettos" (editor's title). From *Nation's Cities*, Vol. 6, No. 10 (October, 1968). Excerpted and reprinted by permission of *Nation's Cities*, the magazine of the National League of Cities, copyright © 1968.

Critics have questioned such tax-credit proposals on the ground that each tax dollar of tax credit increases the budget deficit by as much as a dollar of new spending.

But in this case, it wouldn't work that way. In the first place, those put on payrolls or unemployment rolls will be taken off of welfare rolls or unemployment compensation rolls; and in the second place, as industry is moved into the job-training field, government can be moved out of it.

The Job Corps, for example, has proved a costly failure. It costs some $10,000 a year to train a Job Corpsman for a job that often turns out not to exist. Under the proposed Republican-sponsored Human Investment Act, industry itself—which creates the jobs— would be training men at far less cost for jobs that did exist.

I also have recommended the creation—immediately—of a National Computer Job Bank.

Under this plan, computers would be located in areas of high unemployment, both urban and rural. These would be programmed with data on available jobs and job training programs—locally, statewide, and nationwide. A jobless man could tell the computer operator his employment background, his skills, his job needs—and in minutes he could learn where to find the work or the training he seeks.

These economic programs all are simple in concept and modest in cost. They lack the drama of a $2 billion or a $20 billion price tag. But they are aimed at enlisting the real engines of American progress: individual initiative, private capital, voluntary services—the dynamic four-fifths of our economy *not* accounted for by government.

Tax incentives—whether direct credits, accelerated depreciation or a combination of the two—also should be provided to those businesses that locate branch offices or new plants in poverty areas, whether in the core cities or in rural America.

Free enterprise goes where the profits are. Tax incentives can place these profits where the people are, and where the need is.

I include rural America in this incentive program for two reasons:

The first is need. We don't see rural America exploding on television, but these harsh realities cannot be overlooked: More than half the Americans living below the poverty line live in rural America. Unemployment on the farm is twice what it is in the city. More than half the nation's inadequate housing is in rural areas.

The second reason is, quite simply, that many of the cities' problems are rooted in rural decay. As workers are forced off the farms, they crowd into the cities—often as unprepared for city life as they are for city jobs. To the extent that new jobs can be opened in rural America, to that extent will the pressure be lessened on the cities.

In the ghetto, providing jobs is an essential first step—but this by itself is not enough. Jobs have to be made available within a framework that establishes the pride, the dignity, and the independence of the black American as well as the white. We have to lift the ceiling from black aspirations—essential to this is the encouraging of more ownership, more black control over the destinies of black people.

If black and white are to be brought together indeed, the light of hope has to be brought to the ghetto. If we are to do this, we have to show by example that the American opportunity is neither black nor a white opportunity, but an equal opporunity—and to make this opportunity real, we have to begin in the ghetto itself, where the people are and where the need is.

To assist in this, we need new incentives to get capital flowing into the ghetto. We need both technical and financial assistance for the starting of new black businesses and the expansion of existing ones. We need new institutions that can be the channels of enterprise.

What we have to do is to get private enterprise into the ghetto, and get the people of the ghetto into private enterprise—not only as workers, but as managers and owners.

ALTERNATIVES TO THE GILDED GHETTO

John F. Kain
Joseph J. Persky

Ghetto job creation and other programs aimed at increasing public and private investment in the ghetto have been termed "ghetto gilding" by some opponents of these programs. John F. Kain and Joseph J. Persky argue that ghetto gilding is both inefficient and inimical to a long-run solution to the problems of the ghetto. Joseph Persky is a visiting professor at Fisk University and a part-time staff member of the National Bureau of Economic Research.

Nothing less than a complete change in the structure of the metropolis will solve the problem of the ghetto. It is therefore ironic that current programs which ostensibly are concerned with the welfare of urban Negroes are willing to accept, and are even based on, the permanence of central ghettos. Thus, under every heading of social welfare legislation—education, income transfer, employment, and housing—we find programs that can only serve to strengthen the ghetto and the serious problems that it generates. In particular, these programs concentrate on beautifying the fundamentally ugly structure of the current metropolis and not on providing individuals with the tools necessary to break out of that structure. The shame of the situation is that viable alternatives *do* exist.

Thus, in approaching the problems of Negro employment, first steps could be an improved information system at the disposal of Negro job seekers, strong training programs linked to job placement in industry, and improved transit access between central ghettos and outlying employment areas. Besides the direct effects of such programs on

From "Alternatives to the Gilded Ghetto" by John F. Kain and Joseph J. Persky, *The Public Interest*, No. 14 (Winter, 1969), pp. 74–87. Excerpted and reprinted by permission of *The Public Interest* and the authors. Copyright © 1969 by National Affairs, Inc.

unemployment and incomes, they have the added advantage of encouraging the dispersion of the ghetto and not its further concentration. For example, Negroes employed in suburban areas distant from the ghetto have strong incentives to reduce the time and cost of commuting by seeking out residences near their work places. Frequent informal contact with white coworkers will both increase their information about housing in predominantly white residential areas and help to break down the mutual distrust that is usually associated with the process of integration.

Prospects of housing desegregation would be much enhanced by major changes in urban renewal and housing programs. Current schemes accept and reinforce some of the worst aspects of the housing market. Thus, even the best urban renewal projects involve the government in drastically reducing the supply (and thereby increasing the cost) of low income housing—all this at great expense to the taxpayer. At best there is an implicit acceptance of the alleged desire of the poor to remain in central city slums. At worst, current programs could be viewed as a concerted effort to maintain the ghetto. The same observation can be made about public housing programs. The Commission on Civil Rights in its report on school segregation concluded that government policies for low cost housing were "further reinforcing the trend toward racial and economic separation in metropolitan areas."

An alternative approach would aim at drastically expanding the supply of low income housing *outside* the ghetto. Given the high costs of reclaiming land in central areas, subsidies equivalent to existing urban renewal expenditures for use anywhere in the metropolitan area would lead to the construction of many more units. The new mix by type and location would be likely to favor small, single-family homes and garden apartments on the urban periphery. Some overbuilding would be desirable, the object being the creation of a glut in the low income suburban housing market. It is hard to imagine a situation that would make developers and renters less sensitive to skin color.

These measures would be greatly reinforced by programs that increase the effective demand of Negroes for housing. Rent subsidies to individuals are highly desirable, because they represent the transfer of purchasing power that can be used anywhere in the metropolitan area. Other income transfer programs not specifically tied to housing would have similar advantages in improving the prospects of ghetto dispersal. Vigorous enforcement of open housing statutes would aid the performance of the "impersonal" market, perhaps most importantly by providing developers, lenders, and realtors with an excuse to act in their own self interest.

SUBURBANIZATION OF THE NEGRO

Even in the face of continuing practices of residential segregation, the suburbanization of the Negro can still continue apace. It is important to realize that the presence of Negroes in the suburbs does not necessarily imply Negro integration into white residential neighborhoods. Suburbanization of the Negro and housing integration are not synonymous. Many of the disadvantages of massive, central ghettos would be overcome if they were replaced or even augmented by smaller, dispersed Negro *communities*. Such a pattern would remove the limitations on Negro employment opportunities attributable to the geography of the ghetto. Similarly, the reduced pressure on central city housing markets would improve the prospects for the renewal of middle-income neighborhoods through the operations of the private market. Once the peripheral growth of central city ghettos is checked, the demands for costly investment in specialized, long-distance transport facilities serving central employment areas would be reduced. In addition programs designed to reduce *de facto* school segregation by means of redistributing, bussing, and similar measures would be much more feasible.

Although such a segregated pattern does not represent the authors' idea of a more open society, it could still prove a valuable first step toward the goal. Most groups attempting to integrate suburban neighborhoods have placed great stress on achieving and maintaining some preconceived interracial balance. Because integration is the goal, they feel the need to proceed slowly and make elaborate precautions to avoid "tipping" the neighborhood. The result has been a small, black trickle into all-white suburbs. But if the immediate goal is seen as destroying the ghetto, different strategies should be employed. "Tipping," rather than something to be carefully avoided, might be viewed as a tactic for opening large amounts of suburban housing. If enough suburban neighborhoods are "tipped," the danger of any one of them becoming a massive ghetto would be small.

Education is still another tool that can be used to weaken the ties of the ghetto. Formal schooling plays a particularly important role in preparing individuals to participate in the complex urban society of today. It greatly enhances their ability to compete in the job market with the promise of higher incomes. As a result, large scale programs of compensatory education can make important contributions to a strategy of weakening and eventually abolishing the Negro ghetto. Nevertheless, the important gains of such compensatory programs must be continually weighed against the more general advantages of school desegregation. Where real alternatives exist in the short run, programs consistent with this latter objective should always be chosen. It is important to note that truly effective programs of compensatory education are likely to be extremely expensive and that strategies involving significant amounts of desegregation may achieve the same educational objectives at much lower costs.

Bussing of Negro students may be such a program. Like better access to suburban employment for ghetto job seekers, bussing would weaken the geographic dominance of the ghetto. Just as the informal experience of integration on the job is an important element in changing racial atitudes, integration in the classroom is a powerful learning experience. Insofar as the resistance of suburban communities to accepting low income residents and students is the result of a narrow cost-minimization calculus that attempts to avoid providing public services and in particular education, substantial state and federal subsidies for the education of low income students can prove an effective carrot. Title I programs of the Elementary and Secondary Education Act of 1965 and grants to areas containing large federal installations are precedents. Subsidies should be large enough to cover more than the marginal cost of educating students from low income families, and should make it *profitable* for communities and school districts to accept such students. The experience of the METCO program in Boston strongly suggests that suburban communities can be induced to accept ghetto school children if external sources of financing are available.

Because the above proposals would still leave unanswered some immediate needs of ghetto residents, a strong argument can be made for direct income transfers. Although certain constraints on the use of funds, for example rent supplements, might be maintained, the emphasis should be on providing resources to individuals and not on freezing them into geographic areas. The extent to which welfare schemes are currently tied to particular neighborhoods or communities should be determined, and these programs should be altered so as to remove such limitations on mobility. Keeping in mind the crucial links between the ghetto and the rural South, it is essential that the Southern Negro share in these income transfers.

THE GHETTO AND THE NATION

Although there are major benefits to be gained by both the Negro community and the metropolis at large through a dispersal of the central ghetto, these benefits cannot be realized and are likely to be hindered by programs aimed at making the ghetto a more livable place. In addition to the important objections discussed so far, there is the very real possibility that such programs will run afoul of major migration links with the Negro population of the South. A striking example of this problem can be seen in the issue of ghetto job creation, one of the most popular proposals to improve the ghetto.

Although ghetto job creation, like other "gilding" programs, might initially reduce Negro unemployment, it must eventually affect the system that binds the Northern ghetto to the rural and urban areas of the South. This system will react to any sudden changes in employment and income opportunities in Northern ghettos. If there are no offsetting improvements in the South, the result will be increased rates of migration into still restricted ghetto areas. While we need to know much more than we now do about the elasticity of migration to various economic improvements, the direction of the effect is clear. Indeed it is possible that more than one migrant would appear in the ghetto for every job created. Even at lower levels of sensitivity, a strong wave of in-migration could prove extremely harmful to many other programs. The South in 1960 still accounted for about 60 per cent of the country's Negro population, more than half of which lived in nonmetropolitan areas. In particular, the number of *potential* migrants from the rural South has not declined greatly in recent years.

* * *

Although the differential in white and Negro migration is clearly related to differential economic opportunity, the over-all level of Southern out-migration must be ascribed to the underdeveloped nature of the region. A more rapid pace of Southern economic development could change these historic patterns of Negro migration. Tentative research findings indicate that both manufacturing growth and urbanization in the South reduce Negro out-migration. Although the holding effect of these changes is not so strong for Negroes as for whites, the difference between the two responses can be substantially narrowed. If development took place at a higher rate, the job market would tighten and thus encourage Negroes to stay. Moreover, the *quid pro quo* for large scale subsidies for Southern development might be strong commitments to hire Negro applicants. A serious program of Southern development is worthwhile in its own right as a cure to a century of imbalance in the distribution of economic activity in the nation. From the narrow viewpoint of the North, however, the economic development of the South can play a crucial role in providing leverage in the handling of metropolitan problems.

Belated recognition of the problems created for Northern metropolitan areas by these large-scale streams of rural migration have led in recent months to a large number of proposals to encourage development in rural areas. Not surprisingly the Department of Agriculture has been quick to seize the opportunities provided. A "rural renaissance" has been its response. Full-page advertisements headed, "To save our cities, We must have rural-urban balance," have appeared in a large number of magazines under the aegis of the National Rural Electric Cooperative Association. These proposals invariably fail to recognize that Negro migration from the rural South differs in important respects from rural-urban migration and has different consequences. Failing as they do to distinguish between beneficial and potentially disruptive migration, these proposals for large-scale programs to keep people on the farms, everywhere, are likely to lead to great waste and inefficiency, while failing to come to grips with the problem that motivated the original concern.

IMPROVING SKILLS

A second important approach to easing the pressure on the ghetto is to improve the educational and skill level of incoming migrants. An investment in the under-utilized human resource represented by the Southern white and Negro will pay off in either an expanded Southern economy or a Northern metropolitan job market. Indeed, it is just this flexibility that makes programs oriented to individuals so attractive in comparison to programs oriented to geography. To the extent that a potential migrant can gain skills in demand, his integration into the metropolis, North or South, is that much eased. In light of these benefits, progress in Southern schools has been pitifully slow. Southern Negro achievement levels are the lowest for any group in the country. Southern states with small tax bases and high fertility rates have found it expedient in the past to spend as little as possible on Negro education. Much of the rationalization for this policy is based on the fact that a large proportion of Southern Negroes will migrate and thus deprive the area of whatever educational investment is made in them. This fact undoubtedly has led to some underinvestment in the education of Southern whites as well, but the brunt has been borne by the Negro community.

Clearly it is to the advantage of those areas that are likely to receive these migrants to guarantee their ability to cope with an urban environment. This would be in sharp contrast to migrants who move to the ghetto dependent on the social services of the community and unable to venture into the larger world of the metropolis. Nor are the impacts of inadequate Southern education limited to the first generation of Negro migrants. Parents ill-equipped to adjust to complex urban patterns are unlikely to provide the support necessary for preparing children to cope with a hostile environment. The pattern can be clearly seen in the second generation's reaction to life in the ghetto. It is the children of migrants and not the migrants themselves who seem most prone to riot in the city.

Thus, education of potential migrants is of great importance to both the North and South. The value of the investment is compounded by the extent to which the over-all level of Negro opportunity is expanded. In the North, this is dependent on a weakening of the constricting ties of the ghetto. In the South it depends on economic development per se.

CONCLUDING THOUGHTS

This article has considered alternative strategies for the urban ghetto in light of the strong economic and social link of that community to the metropolis in which it is imbedded and to the nation as a whole. In particular the analysis has centered on the likely repercussions of "gilding programs."

Included prominently among these programs are a variety of proposals designed to attract industry to metropolitan ghettos. There have also been numerous proposals for massive expenditures on compensatory education, housing, welfare, and the like. Model cities programs must be included under this rubric. All such proposals aim at raising the employment, incomes, and well-being of ghetto residents, *within* the existing framework of racial discrimination.

Much of the political appeal of these programs lies in their ability to attract support from a wide spectrum ranging from white separatists, to liberals, to advocates of black power. However, there is an overriding objection to this approach. "Gilding" programs must accept as given a continued growth of Negro ghettos, ghettos which are directly or indirectly responsible for the failure of urban renewal, the crisis in central city finance, urban transportation problems, Negro unemployment, and the inadequacy of metropolitan school systems. Ghetto gilding programs, apart from being objectionable on moral grounds, accept a very large cost in terms of economic inefficiency, while making the solution of many social problems inordinately difficult.

A final objection is that such programs may not work at all, if pursued in isolation. The ultimate result of efforts to increase Negro incomes or reduce Negro unemployment in central city ghettos may be simply to induce a much higher rate of migration of Negroes from Southern rural areas. This will accelerate the already rapid growth of black ghettos, complicating the already impressive list of urban problems.

Recognition of the migration link between Northern ghettos and Southern rural areas has led in recent months to proposals to subsidize economic development, educational opportunities, and living standards in rural areas. It is important to clarify the valuable, but limited, contributions well-designed programs of this kind can make to the problems of the metropolitan ghetto. Anti-migration and migrant improvement programs cannot in themselves improve conditions in Northern ghettos. They cannot overcome the prejudice, discrimination, low incomes, and lack of education that are the underlying "causes" of ghetto unrest. At best they are complementary to programs intended to deal directly with ghetto problems. Their greatest value would be in permitting an aggressive assault on the problems of the ghetto —their role is that of a counterweight which permits meaningful and large scale programs within *metropolitan* areas.

What form should this larger effort take? It would seem that ghetto dispersal is the only strategy that promises a long-run solution. In support of this contention we have identified three important arguments:

1. None of the other programs will reduce the distortions of metropolitan growth and loss of efficiency that result from the continued rapid expansion of "massive" Negro ghettos in metropolitan areas.

2. Ghetto dispersal programs would generally lower the costs of achieving many objectives that are posited by ghetto improvement or gilding schemes.

3. As between ghetto gilding and ghetto dispersal strategies, only the latter is consistent with stated goals of American society.

The conclusion is straightforward. Where alternatives exist, and it has been a major effort of this article to show that they do exist, considerable weight must be placed on their differential impact on the ghetto. Programs that tend to strengthen this segregated pattern should generally be rejected in favor of programs that achieve the same objectives while weakening the ghetto. Such a strategy is not only consistent with the nation's long-run goals, but will often be substantially cheaper in the short run.

DESEGREGATED HOUSING: WHO PAYS
FOR THE REFORMERS' IDEAL?

Frances Fox Piven
Richard A. Cloward

The desirability of integration as both a long- and short-term goal has been largely unquestioned by those interested in improving the position of the Negro American. In their article, Mssrs. Piven and Cloward argue that the efforts to achieve open housing have been a failure and have imposed heavy costs on poor Negroes and whites. They contend that advocates of desegregation should, temporarily at least, redirect their energies toward larger appropriations for low income housing as a way of providing decent ghetto housing. Frances Fox Piven and Richard A. Cloward are regular contributors to liberal opinion magazines and teach at the Columbia University School of Social Work.

Despite the huge congressional majorities enjoyed by President Johnson in the 89th Congress, not much was done for the slums of our cities. Some promising legislation was enacted: the Housing Act of 1965, the rent supplement bill, the demonstration cities bill. But in each case the issue of racial integration endangered the passage of bills, then emasculated them by the meagerness of appropriations. And now, with the 90th Congress, we have probably lost the small margins by which most of the housing legislation survived. Indeed, we may forfeit the small gains already made. It is time, therefore, to re-examine the relation, if any, between racial dispersion and decent housing for the slum poor.

Patterns of ethnic and racial separation in urban settlement are age old, but improving slum housing has nevertheless recently come to be associated with the goal of racial desegregation. Restricted

From "Desegregated Housing: Who Pays for the Reformers' Ideal?" by Frances Fox Piven and Richard A. Cloward, *The New Republic* (December 17, 1966), pp. 17–22. Excerpted and reprinted by permission of *The New Republic*, © 1966, Harrison-Blaine of New Jersey, Inc., and the authors.

housing is regarded by reformers as the key factor in creating and
maintaining racial barriers, and in turn racial barriers are said to
force Negroes into the deteriorated slum; therefore, it is felt that
desegregation should be a central objective of housing and redevel-
opment programs for the poor. But since there is, at best, little public
support for low-income housing programs, and this tenuous support
has been overwhelmed by fierce opposition to residential integra-
tion, the struggle for residential integration has cost the poor, espe-
cially the Negro poor, dearly.

In effect, the desperate need for better housing and facilities in the
ghetto has been and continues to be sacrificed to the goal of residential
integration—a goal which, given the political realities of racial con-
flict in urban areas, can only be said to be receding from view. And
as this goal recedes, so too does decent low-income housing.

Consider the magnitude of our failure both to provide low-income
housing *and* to desegregate ghettoes. Despite the Housing Act of
1949, in which Congress asserted a national responsibility to pro-
vide a decent dwelling for every family, the lack of good housing
for the poor in our big cities has grown. In the three decades since
the federal public-housing program was initiated, only 600,000 low-
income dwelling units have been built. In less than half that time,
the federal urban-renewal program and the federal highway pro-
gram have together demolished close to 700,000 units, most of them
low rental. Private builders, spurred on by federal tax incentives and
mortgage programs, have made further inroads on the supply of low-
income housing by reclaiming slum land to erect middle- and upper-
income units. As a result, the dislocated poor are crowded into residual
ghetto areas and deterioration accelerates. . . .

Not only has the supply of low-income units diminished, but seg-
regation has increased! Nor is there any reason to believe that this
trend will abate. For one thing, differential birthrates reinforce exist-
ing patterns of segregation, concentrating larger and larger numbers
of Negroes wherever they live. . . . During the decade which ended
in 1960, the nonwhite population in American cities increased by
half, urban whites by one-fourth.

As the urban Negro population rises, segregation is intensified.
The most dramatic separation by color *within* the urban area has
taken place between the central city and suburban ring. . . . Cen-
tral cities now contain less than half the urban white population, but
80 per cent of urban nonwhites. . . .

WHAT WOULD INTEGRATION REQUIRE?

In view of these trends, the task of maintaining racial balance in the
city seems insuperable; to offset them, huge numbers of families would

have to be shuffled about by desegregation programs. This point was spelled out last spring by George Schermer. . . . Schermer estimated the numbers of people who would have to be moved each year in order to insure a 50–50 population balance in Washington, D.C. in the year 2000. Assuming that migration trends and birthrates remain constant, 12,000 nonwhite families would have to be dispersed to suburban areas and 4,000 white families induced to return to the District *every year until 2000.*

Even if whites could be induced back to the city and Negroes accommodated in the suburbs, residential integration would not result. For within the central city itself, residential concentration by color is on the upswing. . . .

Again, assuming that present trends persist, Schermer estimates that to achieve integration neighborhood-by-neighborhood in Philadelphia by the end of the century, 6,000 Negro families would have to go to the suburbs and 3,000 whites settle *exclusively in ghetto areas* each year. The numbers, of course, would be infinitely greater in cities like New York and Chicago, which have much larger aggregations of Negroes. . . .

Our experience with a variety of approaches to desegregating housing has not been in the least encouraging. The most popular approach is legal reforms, coupled with information and education programs. Legislation is sought which prohibits prejudicial treatment of Negroes, whether by deed restrictions, by discriminatory actions of private realtors or landlords, or by governmental policies themselves (such as the FHA mortgage underwriting policy, rescinded in 1945, which prescribed racially homogeneous housing). These reforms reflect an essentially libertarian ideal: a legal structure which ensures the individual rights of minority group members. But it is by now self-evident that such reforms have little actual impact on urban segregation in housing (or in education or employment).

* * *

Part of the reason that legal reforms have had little effect is the weakness of the laws themselves. Many of the discriminatory acts which produce segregation in private housing involve the sacred precincts of property and domicile. Efforts to protect by law the rights of minorities shade into infringements of the rights of others and may even be contrary to other laws which protect rights of property and privacy.

Legal reforms are further weakened by the reluctance to provide for effective enforcement. New York has both a State Commission on Human Rights and a parallel City Commission. The procedures for securing redress, however, ordinarily require knowledge and patience on the part of the plaintiff which cannot in fairness be expected of someone merely looking for a decent place to live. Moreover, although one apartment may be "opened" after tortuous procedures, there is no deterrence to further violations, no carryover effect. Each negotiated enforcement of the law remains an isolated event, and so members of a minority have little confidence in the efficacy of registering complaints. . . .

Broad educational efforts are intended to change discriminatory attitudes in the white community. "Fair-housing committees" in receiving communities are intended to overcome hostility toward entering Negroes. Information and broker services are designed to remedy communication gaps, such as lack of information about housing opportunities outside the ghetto and difficulties in gaining access for inspection. The Urban League's "Operation Open City" combines all these strategies to help Negro families find housing.

Housing opportunities are still, however, overwhelmingly controlled by the regular institutions of the private real-estate market, and the mores of the market have been only incidentally affected by legal advances and desegregation programs. Private real-estate agents reflect the inclinations of the vast majority of housing consumers, and so they distribute information concerning available housing and provide access for inspection in ways that accord with existing class and racial neighborhood patterns. Projects like Operation Open City and fair-housing committees have at best opened just a few housing opportunities beyond the ghetto. . . . Furthermore, these efforts reach predominantly middle-class Negroes: housing in outlying communities generally requires at least a lower-middle income. The ghetto poor are restricted by white neighborhoods generally, but the most furious opposition comes from white working-class neighborhoods—the very ones with housing many Negroes might be able to afford.

IF NEGROES HAD MORE MONEY

Eliminating the poverty of the ghetto masses is the basis of a second general approach to residential integration. Proceeding from our belief in individual opportunity and the "open" society, the argument is that Negroes will be able to bid competitively for housing outside the ghetto once they have better jobs and incomes. There are a number of fallacies here.

First, programs intended to advance Negroes economically—by education and job training—currently reach a mere one in 10 of America's poor, white as well as Negro. Even if the scope of these programs were vastly expanded, millions of the poor would still not be helped. Of the 35 million people below the federal poverty line (*e.g.*, $3,000 per annum for an urban family of four), several million are aged and are permanently unemployable. One-third of the poor are in families headed by females, and it does not seem reasonable to expect this group to raise itself from poverty by entering the labor force. Many of the remaining poor are ill; others are permanently noncompetitive for a host of additional reasons, not the least being the debilitating effects of years of chronic unemployment and underemployment.

More than half of the poor are under 18. Presumably the optimists who advocate skills-enhancement as a solution to poverty have the potential of this group in mind. But in the past, the upward journey to the middle class has taken low-income groups as much as three generations. Negroes are handicapped at the outset by chronic deprivation; they confront persisting barriers of economic and social discrimination; they must surmount new barriers posed by automation and the professionalization of occupations. Under the cirmumstances, they can hardly be expected to lift themselves, one by one, more rapidly than members of groups before them which had much greater economic opportunity. For most poor of the present generation, and perhaps for many in the next, a strategy of individual mobility is irrelevant.

Even if large numbers of Negroes are lifted either to or somewhat above the poverty line, their chance of getting decent housing will not greatly improve. In urban areas, adequate housing is hard to come by for families with annual incomes of less than $7,000; in 1960, only 3.4 per cent of Negroes had such incomes. Indeed, middle-class whites have obtained huge governmental subsidies to bring decent housing within their reach (e.g., urban-renewal land write-downs, low-cost government-insured mortgages, special federal tax advantages for builders and realtors, as well as local tax abatements).

Furthermore, because of discriminatory patterns, Negroes, in effect, pay more for housing than whites. Although in most metropolitan areas Negroes pay slightly lower rentals than whites in each income group, they get vastly inferior housing. Income gains will continue to be partly dissipated in excessive rentals.

We must also stress that resistance in the receiving community persists, whatever the incomes of potential Negro invaders. In a recent book, *Negroes in Cities,* Karl and Alma Taeuber conclude after extensive analysis of census data that "residential segregation prevails regardless of the relative economic status of the white and Negro resident."

CONSEQUENCES OF OUR GOOD INTENTIONS

The myth that integrationist measures are bringing better housing to the Negro poor comforts liberals; it placates (and victimizes) the Negro masses; and it antagonizes and arouses the bulk of white Americans. The "backlash" is part of its legacy. While turmoil rages over

integration, housing conditions worsen. They worsen partly because
the solution continues to be defined in terms of desegregation, so that
the energies and attention of reformers are diverted from attempts to
ameliorate housing in the ghetto itself.

By being linked to the goal of integration, traditional programs
for low-income housing (*e.g.*, public housing) have become so con-
troversial that appropriations are kept low and in many places are
not even used. Although the 1949 Housing Act alone authorized
810,000 units of low-rent housing, a mere 600,000 units have been
constructed since the first National Housing Act in 1937. During the
past few years, we have constructed only about 26,000 units annually
or about half of what could have been built under existing legislation.
The ghetto poor have paid in this way for the struggle over whether
Negro and white shall mingle, neighborhood by neighborhood.

Public housing was intended, by at least some of its proponents,
to facilitate integration as a by-product of rehousing the poor. And
it has always been plagued by that secondary goal. Integrated projects
have been thwarted because, as Negroes move in, low-income whites
leave or are reluctant to apply. (The Federal Public Housing Agency
classifies only 27 per cent of its projects as integrated and these in-
clude an unspecified number which have only one or two Negro
families.) The resulting high-rise brick ghettos offend liberals, and
they attack. But when housing officials attempt to bring about integra-
tion by such devices as quota systems, other critics are offended on
the ground that such procedures are discriminatory. . . .

Efforts to further integration by locating housing projects in white
neighborhoods have provoked far more serious opposition than efforts
to integrate the projects themselves. Only when white tenants pre-
dominate is there any degree of tolerance for public housing in these
communities. In Newark, for example, the racial balance in projects
ranges from over 90 per cent white in outlying "country club" areas
to over 90 per cent Negro for projects located in central ghetto
wards. Because this accommodation was made from the outset, New-
ark has been able to win support for public housing and hence to
build relatively more units than most other cities. Similarly the New
York City Housing Authority has long accommodated to the wishes of
borough presidents in site selections (and is much criticized for it),
and has also used its full share of public-housing subsidies. But in
many localities, disputes over the location of public-housing projects
have evoked furious controversy, often leading to the reduction of the
program and surely making its political future shaky. In a study of
public-housing decisions in Chicago, Martin Meyerson and Edward
Banfield showed how volatile the site-selection issue is. By proposing
locations which raised the integration issue, the public-housing au-
thority provoked a two-and-a-half-year struggle which not only de-

feated the site proposal but consolidated opposition to public housing itself. . . .

The new rent-supplement law bears the same political onus as public housing. The current appropriation of $20 million will permit only a few showpiece displays. If experience with public housing is any predictor, the opposition which rent supplements provoked in Congress and which almost defeated it will be repeated in each local community as efforts are made to implement the plan. White majorities will veto any project they feel will threaten their neighborhood and will eventually ban the program that raises the threat. Public subsidies, in short, have failed to reverse the trend toward segregation in urban areas and have not produced new or rehabilitated housing for the poor.

The slum ghetto thus remains at the mercy of the real-estate market which controls it. Shunned by stable investors, the ghetto attracts less knowledgeable and less scrupulous speculators who demand high rates of return for dollars expended on so risky and disreputable a venture. The ghetto is left with no stable financial credit—the underbelly of the real-estate market, where profits are made quickly and outside the law by preying on captive tenants. And that profit is wrested by offering an increasingly deteriorated product at increasingly inflated prices.

            *   *   *

Recent housing and redevelopment programs, put forward as attempts to serve "the city as a whole" by clearing slums, improving the tax base, or retrieving the middle class from the suburbs, have had the effect of intensifying ghetto deterioration. We have spent some $3 billion on urban-renewal programs, and in the process whole low-income communities have been destroyed, including some 328,000 units of housing (most of them low rental). Only some 13,000 units of low-rent public housing have been constructed on the area sites. Luxury apartment houses, stadiums, coliseums, auditoriums and office buildings now stand where the poor once lived. (Highway development has had equally devastating effects.) Curiously, these programs are sometimes justified by the goal of integration, for it is hoped they will lure middle-class whites back from the suburbs.

            *   *   *

TAKING ACCOUNT OF WHITE HOSTILITY

The Achilles heel of housing programs has been precisely our insistence that better housing for the black poor be achieved by residential desegregation. This ideal glosses over the importance of the

ethnic community as a staging area for groups to build the communal
solidarity and power necessary to compel eventual access to the
mainstream of urban life. If the ideal of heterogeneity has led reform-
ers to press for measures which threaten to bring Negroes into white
neighborhoods, the force of separatism has consistently won out—
and housing in the ghetto has worsened.

If group conflict is at the root of past failures, strategies must be
found to improve ghetto housing without arousing the ire of powerful
segments of the white community. In managing this conflict, politicians
try to make concessions to contending groups. But this is possible
only if significant groups in the political majority remain unaroused
or relatively indifferent to what has been conceded. As we have
shown, the prospect that Negroes might invade white neighborhoods
generates such intense opposition that politicians, in the interest of
self-preservation, are forced to avoid any action except to promote
token measures to placate reformers. Hostile feelings created by the
struggle over integration tie the hands of political leaders who might
otherwise give their support to less controversial concessions, such as
subsidies for low-income housing in the ghetto.

It seems clear, then, that reformers must apply what political pres-
sure they have to secure relief in the ghetto itself. We already have
the legal and administrative channels, but we have put virtually no
funds into them. The most urgent need is for subsidies, for both new
housing and the interim rehabilitation of existing structures, and for
vigorous intervention in the ownership and management of slum
buildings.

*   *   *

WAYS OF REHABILITATING THE SLUMS

New housing can be built under the public-housing program, or
through the use of rent supplements and low-cost government mort-
gages. These programs do not fix and limit the form of low-rental
housing—public-housing authorities can use their subsidies to buy or
to lease privately built dwellings, for example; they are not restricted
to barren high-rise projects. Because overcrowding is at a critical peak
in most central city ghettoes, new housing should be used to augment
the supply of dwelling units and neighborhood space. We should not
tear down any but the most hazardous slum housing. We should build
either in marginal and underused areas, where it is possible to extend
ghetto boundaries without excessive neighborhood friction, or in more
outlying ghetto enclaves.

Slum housing can also be substantially upgraded by repairs, new
wiring and plumbing (estimated by housing experts at about $1,500

per unit) or gutting and rebuilding a structure (which can cost as much as eight times that amount). Because it is cheaper and does not require neighborhood upheaval, various kinds of rehabilitation should be given priority, even if eventual demolition and rebuilding are contemplated.

*   *   *

A number of minor changes in regulations could multiply our tools for improving ghetto housing. For example, new public housing now costs as much as $22,500 per unit, largely because of extraordinarily high standards of construction required by federal regulations. Archaic and inflexible local building codes encumber new construction and rehabilitation and add substantially to costs. These regulations are not merely vestigial or accidental. They are promoted and protected by the organized groups in the construction and real-estate industries whose interests are served by maintaining traditional and costly methods of building. Even these minor reforms require the mobilizing of political support.

Federal mortgage and grant programs for low-income rehabilitation are now underused, partly because of certain limiting regulations. For instance, federal low-cost mortgages have not been fully exploited (New York City's allotment for the current year is set at $150 million, but much of it is likely to go unused). There are two reasons: only nonprofit or limited profit corporations are eligible, and modest rent supplements are needed in addition to low-cost mortgages in order to yield low rents. Local government could help create such corporations (drawing in churches, settlement houses or community organizations as sponsors); it could provide rent-supplement funds from local revenues (barring any expansion and relaxation of restrictions in the federal rent-supplement program). But none of this is likely to work so long as low-income housing arouses intense local opposition because it is tied to racial integration.

The new demonstration cities bill authorizes $900 million over two years for slum rehabilitation. The legislation is broadly permissive, so that localities can propose a wide variety of programs. (Note that congressional opposition to the bill was only overcome by a last minute amendment barring use of the legislation to promote racial balance.) If liberals follow their accustomed route and force new contests over desegregation, this bill is likely to go the way of earlier housing measures, weakened and mangled at each stage of public decision.

The point, in short, is that if reformers can be persuaded to forfeit for a time the ideal of desegregation, there might be a chance of mustering political support and money for low-income housing. This would be no small achievement.

SUGGESTED READINGS

Abrams, Charles. *Forbidden Neighbors: A Study of Prejudice in Housing.* New York: Harper and Brothers, 1955.

Becker, Gary S. *The Economics of Discrimination.* Chicago: University of Chicago Press, 1957.

Caplovitz, David. *The Poor Pay More: Consumer Practices of Low-Income Families.* New York: The Free Press of Glencoe, Inc., 1963.

Clark, Kenneth B. *Dark Ghetto.* New York: Harper & Row, Inc., 1965.

Dentler, Robert A. "Barriers to Northern School Desegregation," *Daedalus, The Negro American-2* (Winter 1966), 45–63.

Doeringer, Peter B. "Promotion Systems and Equal Employment Opportunity," *Proceedings of the Industrial Relations Research Association* (San Francisco: December 28–29, 1966), 278–289.

Downs, Anthony. "An Economic Analysis of *Property Values and Race,*" *Land Economics,* XXXVI (May 1960), 181.

Duncan, Beverly and Philip M. Hauser. *Housing a Metropolis—Chicago.* New York: The Free Press of Glencoe, Inc., 1960.

Duncan, Otis D. "Discrimination Against Negroes," *Annals of the American Academy of Political and Social Science,* 371 (May 1967), 85–103.

———. "Inheritance of Poverty or Inheritance of Race?" in *On Understanding Poverty: Perspectives from the Social Sciences,* ed. Daniel P. Moynihan. New York: Basic Books, 1969.

——— and Beverly Duncan. *The Negro Population of Chicago—A Study in Residential Succession.* Chicago: The University of Chicago Press, 1957.

Gilman, H. J. "Economic Discrimination and Unemployment," *American Economic Review,* LV: 5 (December 1965), 1077–1096.

Ginzberg, Eli. *The Negro Potential.* New York: Columbia University Press, 1956.

SUGGESTED READINGS   185

Glazer, Nathan, "Is 'Integration' Possible in the New York Schools?," in
American Race Relations Today, ed. Earl Raab. Garden City: Anchor
Books, 1962.

———— and Daniel Patrick Moynihan. *Beyond the Melting Pot: The
Negroes, Puerto Ricans, Jews, Italians and Irish of New York City*.
Cambridge: The M.I.T. Press and Harvard University Press, 1963.

Grier, Eunice and George Grier. "Equality and Beyond: Housing Segrega-
tion in the Great Society," *Daedalus, The Negro American-2* (Winter
1966), 77–106.

Grodzins, Morton. "The Metropolitan Area as a Racial Problem," in
American Race Relations Today, ed. Earl Raab. Garden City: Anchor
Books, 1962.

Handlin, Oscar. *The Newcomers: Negroes and Puerto Ricans in a Chang-
ing Metropolis*. Cambridge: Harvard University Press, 1959.

Hanoch, Giora. "An Economic Analysis of Earning and Schooling," *The
Journal of Human Resources*, II: 3 (Summer 1967), 310–329.

Hauser, Philip M. "Demographic Factors in the Integration of the Negro,"
Daedalus (Fall 1965), 847–878.

Kain, John F. "Housing Segregation, Negro Employment, and Metropolitan
Decentralization," *Quarterly Journal of Economics*, LXXXII: 2 (May
1968), 175–197.

———— and Joseph J. Persky. "The North's Stake in Southern Rural Pov-
erty," *Rural Poverty in the United States*, A Report by the President's
National Advisory Commission on Rural Poverty. Washington, D.C.:
Government Printing Office, 1968.

Killingsworth, Charles C. *Jobs and Income for Negroes*. Ann Arbor, Mich.:
Institute of Labor and Industrial Relations, 1968.

Laurenti, Luigi. *Property Values and Race: Studies in Seven Cities*. Berk-
eley: University of California Press, 1960.

Liebow, Elliot. *Tally's Corner: A Study of Streetcorner Men*. Boston: Little
Brown & Co., 1967.

Marshall, Ray. *The Negro and Organized Labor*. New York: John Wiley &
Sons, 1965.

————. *The Negro Worker*. New York: Random House, 1967.

Myrdal, Gunnar. *An American Dilemma: The Negro Problem and Modern
Democracy*. New York: Harper and Brothers, 1944.

Norgren, Paul H. and Samuel E. Hill. *Toward Fair Employment.* New York: Columbia University Press, 1964.

Northrup, Herbert R. and Richard L. Rowan (eds.). *The Negro and Employment Opportunity: Problems and Practices.* Ann Arbor, Mich.: Bureau of Industrial Relations, 1965.

Rapkin, Chester and William Grigsby. *The Demand for Housing in Racially Mixed Areas.* Berkeley: University of California Press, 1960.

Ross, Arthur M. and Herbert Hill (eds.). *Employment, Race, and Poverty.* New York: Harcourt, Brace & World, Inc., 1967.

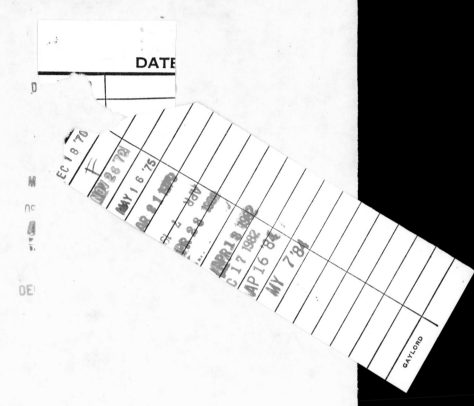